THE OTHER SIDE

VISIT NOW!

By *Geozuwa*

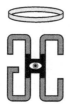

Amethyst Press, Inc.
P.O. Box 5268
Deltona, FL 32728
www.amethystpress.com

Ordering Information:
Quantity sales. Special discounts are available on quantity purchases by corporations, associations, universities, book clubs, and others. For details, contact the publisher at the address above.

ISBN 13: 978-1-943111-00-8

ISBN 10: 1943111006

First Edition 2015

Printed in the United States of America

Author's Intentions

My intentions, infused with Pure Love White Light Healing Energy directly from the Infinite Source of Creation, for all who look upon this page, whether you read the entire book or not:

I want you to enjoy life to the fullest! I want you to live your perfect life of infinite abundance, happiness, and joy with perfect health at all times. I want you to know with absolute certainty that you deserve to be loved perfectly, and to share love perfectly. I want you to be aware that you are always surrounded and protected by Pure Love White Light. I want you to continue to attract good people and good situations into your life. I want you to succeed at everything you do. If there are still lessons for you to learn in this life, I want you to learn them in the quickest, most positive, and most beneficial manner for your highest good and ultimate happiness. I want you to walk along a higher path of Love & Light. I want you to think and act with love at all times, to always flow with infinite intelligence and eternal wisdom. I want you to make all decisions with strength, courage, confidence, clarity of mind, clarity of purpose, and perfect awareness, with pure positive intentions.
May you heal on every level and continue to adjust to your perfection as you read these words.

With All of the Blessings from the Infinite Source of Creation,
Always with Love, Light, & Gratitude,
Geozuwa

iii

I miss you my friend...

I miss our conversations lasting till dawn,
And your silly comments about life you've known;
So, I keep calling you on the phone...
I miss our long walks without true destinations,
And your silent company with no expectations;
So, I throw leaves your way as invitations...
I miss our spontaneous trips filled with excitement,
Although, sometimes, I might seem to be frightened;
So, I set your bag and shoes by the door in alignment...
I miss our evenings with a glass of wine and movie,
Even when I'm watching and all you do is just act goofy;
So, I turn your TV on at night, oh how spooky!
I keep sending messages to you from above,
For you to feel my presence and my love.

***

I miss you my friend...
I wish I could tell you how weird things are now,
I bet you wouldn't stop saying your silly "wow".
My phone is ringing but no number shows,
And when I say "hello" only loud static arose.
In the park, on my lonely walks I now take,
Beautiful creations on the ground the leaves make.
Every morning on the weekends you would not believe,
My traveling bag and shoes are waiting for me to leave.
At evenings when I am ready with a glass of wine to relax,
The TV starts on its own, and the volume rises to its max!
I wish I could talk to you my dear friend,
And have more time with you to spend.
At times, I think you are still around,
I know, I know how crazy this must sound...

–   by Majea Cuantum

Table of Contents

h) Bad Programming
i) Forgiveness

e) Let Go
f) Healing

a) Discover Your Path/Purpose
b) Answers
c) Knowledge/Wisdom
d) Visit with Loved Ones
e) Soul Mates
f) Soul Circle
g) Healing
h) Metaphysical Abilities
i) Oneness of the Universe
j) Evolve Your Soul
k) Pure Love

a) Self-Hypnosis
b) Inner Temple of Creation
c) Astral Travel
d) Dream Control
e) Free from Negative Karma
f) Super-Conscious

a) New You
b) Eternal Home
c) Become Whole
d) Increased Awareness
e) Napoleon
f) Experience for Yourself
g) Visit Now - Without Dying

CHAPTER 1: THE BIG QUESTIONS

"Perhaps they are not stars, but rather openings in heaven where the love of our lost ones pours through and shines down upon us to let us know they are happy"
                                                                -Eskimo Saying

"There are infinite possibilities to each and every infinite possibility."
                                                                - Geozuwa

Have you ever wondered where you go when you die? Have you ever lost a loved one and wished you could still communicate after their passing? Do you wonder if your loved ones can still see you? Have you ever lost someone and never had a chance to, say goodbye, apologize, or let them know that you love them? Have you ever wondered why you were born? Why do you have the parents you have? Did you chose your parents? Did you chose to live the life that you are living before you were even born? Are you on your right path?

Like most people, you have probably heard thousands of ideas and beliefs as to what happens to you when you die. These ideas and beliefs are from individuals, or groups of people, who have been taught certain concepts, mostly inspired by religious teachings, who continue to pass it down through generations. Maybe you have narrowed it down to a select few ideas with an openness to varying possibilities. However, like most people, you probably do not know with absolute certainty what happens when you die. You may have unwavering faith of a life after death, and truly believe that you know with absolute certainty that it exists, but my contention is that to truly KNOW something exists is to experience it for yourself.

If you believe in a life after death you may still wonder if your loved ones can see and hear you. Perhaps you have had a "feeling", at least once in your life, that your loved one was present after passing. Maybe you have had a "dream" immediately before awakening in which your loved one was communicating with you. Was there ever a brief moment in which you thought you heard your loved one saying your name? If you did indeed experience some of these occurrences it may have strengthened your belief in the Other Side. However, if you are like most people you may have chalked these experiences up to your mind or imagination. Psychologists may say that your mind created these experiences for you to cope with the passing of a loved one. If there is an opening for any amount of doubt, regardless of how slight it may be, it is not the same as KNOWing something with absolute certainty.

Usually when someone close dies unexpectedly there can be many psychological and emotional effects. If a loved one's passing is a complete surprise, you may be left with so many feelings and emotions of the sudden loss that can, according to psychologists, trigger certain hallucinations, feelings, and auditory occurrences regarding your loved one. Perhaps a psychologist may convince you that your mind, in an attempt to cope with the sudden loss, is making you believe in things that are not 'actually' happening. The psychologist may be correct in certain situations. The mind is very powerful and can create such occurrences. However, it does not definitively mean those situations are not real. Your loved one may indeed be attempting to communicate with you, at minimum, to let you know that they are still alive, just in a different form of life. Would it not be great if you could visit with them on the Other Side? Would you like to know if certain occurrences in your life were real and it was either a loved one or a Spirit Guide behind those events?

Many times the mind, from a point of overwhelming guilt, can create scenarios of visitations and dreams of loved ones who have passed. It is possible, from a psychological perspective, that if your last words spoken to a close family relative shortly before their passing were said in anger you may be filled with guilt. Not having a chance to apologize, especially when you did not really mean the words spoken, could weigh heavy on your mind thus allowing the mind to manifest from the state and emotions of guilt. Although I can tell you right now that your loved one forgives you and understands what had taken place, would it not be a wonderful feeling to hear it directly from them, face to face, while visiting them on the Other Side?

There may have be times in your life you had wondered if you made the right choices. You may have always dreamed about doing something different with your life, but something or someone steered you into a different direction. Were there moments in your life when you asked yourself why things have happened in your life? Have you ever wondered, like most people, at certain points in life, what is the purpose of it all? Have you ever asked yourself if there is a purpose to your existence?

"Who am I? Where do I come from? Why am I here? Where am I going?" Most people go their entire lives without having these questions ever answered. I am here to tell you that, not only can you have all of your questions answered, but you can experience the 'Other Side' now. You can visit the Other Side now and receive all of the answers to all of your questions firsthand! You can attain a beautiful and powerful state of Knowing! You can easily learn to visit the Other Side whenever you wish to. You can learn and quickly master bringing yourself to the higher states of awareness to vividly communicate with your Spirit Guides whenever you need. Would it not be wonderful, especially when you are at a serious crossroads in your life, faced with a significant life decision concerning your career, health, finances, children, parents, love, relationships, and any one of the many choices that can define a lifetime, to be able to ask your Guardian Angels or a loved one for guidance? It is easy to receive the answers and guidance for the best choices with the most beneficial outcomes when consulting with higher evolved intelligent entities, on the Other Side, who have an unconditional love for you with only the purest, most positive, intentions for you.

Throughout this book I will share with you my personal experiences and knowledge to bring you closer to an understanding and awareness of a beautiful, amazing place of perfection where you have originated from and where you are going when you depart this "physical" world. Of course, I will answer most, if not all, of your questions starting with, yes there is so much more to this world and life than what you have been taught. Yes, there is a beautiful place of Pure Love, absolute forgiveness, complete happiness and joy into which you will go when you leave this world, where your loved ones who have passed have gone. Yes, there is absolutely life after death and life before birth!

You may have read other books on this subject. You may have been told by a priest, a rabbi, any cleric, or any teacher of faith, about the Other Side and how to get there. You may have been taught what to do in this life to ensure your entrance to the Other Side. Whatever religion you were born into, whatever religion you practice or do not practice, has no bearing on 'how' or 'if' you will go to the Other Side. Almost everything taught is how to ensure your entrance to that beautiful perfect place when you die. I am here to tell you that you do not have to wait to die to visit the Other Side. You do not have to die to experience the Pure Love Bliss of the Other Side. You do not have to die to communicate with your loved ones who have passed.

Throughout this book I will present to you with an abundance of evidence from personal, and professional, experiences of the existence of life after death. You will learn that I have gone to the Other Side, almost every day, since early childhood, and you will learn of some of the countless clients and students whom I have guided to the Other Side and back. I will present, from my own experiences, and my family members' experiences, a perspective providing you with an understanding that you are not alone. Your loved ones can see you and are very aware of your situations, and are awaiting your return to your true home on the Other Side. And most importantly, you will discover how easy it is for you to visit the Other Side now.

I am writing this book to offer to you a unique opportunity to visit the Other Side in person. This book is an invitation for you to experience, firsthand, the Pure Love, joy, and perfection of the Other Side. I am inviting you to receive all of the answers to all of your questions, not just from me or any other teachers, but on your own directly from the Source. This is an invitation for you to become aware with absolute certainty that your soul is eternal and you continue to exist when your physical body dies. You do not have to visit any mediums or psychics. After reading this book you will know how you can easily and effortlessly journey to the Other Side anytime you wish on your own.

Reading this book will assist you in opening up more to accept the reality of life after death. You will discover that once you are open and more accepting of the possibility it makes it much easier to be aware of your loved ones and spirit guides who will, often, try to communicate with you. You know that sometimes

6

in the waking conscious state if you are not paying attention, and someone is trying to speak to you, you do not even hear them, regardless of how close they are to you. The same applies to the open communication with all of the loving beings on the Other Side - it is very possible when one is open to it. If a person is not open to the idea of life after death, and the ease of communication, it makes it more difficult to hear or see. This book will assist you in breaking down those walls and barriers.

You have Spirit Guides/Guardian Angels watching over you, helping you, and guiding you along your path. I wish to impart this knowledge to you, not just by opening you up to more possibilities, but to experience firsthand for yourself, being face to face with your Spirit Guides. Discover your path, your purpose, the truth of your existence and your infinite potential!

Maybe you have read, or heard of, accounts of people who have had near-death experiences. Most of those individuals came back with extraordinary gifts and knowledge. You do not have to have a near-death experience to receive the same gifts or knowledge. After reading this book you will be aware that it is possible to receive all of the knowledge and wisdom of the entire Universe, and to gain extraordinary, amazing, and powerful gifts and abilities without dying. This book is an invitation to not just read about it, to not just dream about it, to not just hope for it with faith alone. This book is an invitation to experience it firsthand!

CHAPTER 2: MY EARLY EXPERIENCES

"When you hold your baby in your arms the first time, and you think of all the things you can say and do to influence him, it's a tremendous responsibility. What you do with him can influence not only him, but everyone he meets and not for a day or a month or a year but for time and eternity"
-Rose Kennedy

"Every child should be guided to think and act, for themselves, with love and pure positive intentions."
-Geozuwa

My early experiences grew from stories from my family that, even if I did not have my own experiences, would influence my beliefs in an afterlife. Having my own adventures in the metaphysical allowed me not only to believe that death was not the end, but it gave me a powerful "Knowing" that our Souls are eternal. First, I will share some of my family's stories.

My grandmother Gerry's favorite uncle gave her a large antique porcelain clock shortly before he passed away. She kept this family heirloom even though the clock did not work. Through the years, the clock that never worked, would chime every time a person in the family or a close friend of the family died. Not only did the clock never work, but the chiming mechanism was missing!

My careless uncle, Grandma Gerry's son, had accidentally shattered the clock into several pieces a couple of years before my grandfather Frank had passed. Grandma Gerry, never disposing the clock, kept the pieces in a pile in the corner of their bedroom. When my grandfather was in the hospital dying the doorbell would continue to ring sporadically and occasionally the dog would bark at the clock pieces in the corner. The moment of my grandfather's passing the doorbell rang, non-stop, and the dog barked for thirty minutes at the clock pieces, I witnessed these events firsthand.

When my mother was fifteen years old, sleeping on the couch in my grandmother's home, she was awakened by a woman in the middle of the night. This woman had my mother get a pen and paper and write down important dates for her to give to her father's mother, my great-grandmother Josephine. The next morning in my family's flower shop, below her apartment, my mother noticed a picture on the wall in the back room that she had never noticed before. She immediately informed her mother that the woman in the picture was in their home the night before and described the whole visit. My grandmother explained to her that it was her great-grandmother Angelina who had died before she was born. Years later all of the dates corresponded to personal family tragedies!

This event, alone, should push a person in the direction of believing that there is life after death. This experience that my mother had as a teenager would indicate that, not only is there life after death, but that our loved ones can communicate with us. It shows that our loved ones are watching over us and in special circumstances, they can, and will, if necessary, warn us against certain choices and events.

As Grandma Gerry was working in the flower shop one day a voice whispered in her ear that her children were in danger at the beach. No one was near her, but the voice urgently told her to hurry to a specific point at the beach. My mother and my two uncles were in their early teens and were supposed to be in school when my grandmother received this warning. My grandfather insisted that they were in school, but my grandmother was persistent. They drove to the exact location of the beach that the voice had warned, to discover that my mother and my two uncles were surrounded by a gang. They had arrived at the exact moment to stave off the serious violence that was about to erupt!

There are infinite possibilities as to why and how Grandma Gerry received this warning. It is possible that her Spirit Guide or one of her children's Spirit Guides, or even a loved one who had passed, whispered in her ear. Again, we are not alone. We are being watched over from the Other Side. There are events in this life that may happen that are not, or were not, meant to happen. And our loved ones or Spirit Guides will intercede with messages, signs, and, even, visits. Many times, unfortunately, those signs or messages will go unheeded. People just brush the signs or messages aside to confirm that they are not crazy. It would have only taken a split second for Grandma Gerry to say to herself that the whisper was nonsense and continued to wash the dishes. It took courage for her to persist with my grandfather and make him take her to the beach to rescue her children.

Throughout my childhood and well into my adult life I had experienced several para-normal occurrences and other worldly visitations in my grandparent's building and flower shop. Some of the events included the lights going on and off by themselves, the water turning on, the door bell ringing and knocking with no physical being present, our names being called, we were tapped on, and tugged at, and the television turning on, and so much more!

One night in my early adulthood I was sleeping in the family's flower shop. Around midnight the locks, including the deadbolt, on the front door continued to turn, making the locking and unlocking sounds. The door was glass and I had a clear view that there was no one there. The noises interrupted my sleep periodically throughout the night. It did not disturb me much, however, because I was accustomed to the supernatural, the "ghosts", and the happenings in this building.

Around 5 a.m. banging sounds were coming from the back room. At first I was ignoring the sounds attempting to return to sleep. The banging was progressively getting louder. Then I thought that perhaps someone was trying to break in! I jumped out of bed and cautiously made my way to investigate. Nearing the work room, a room before the back, the banging increased in intensity and frequency. Upon entering the work room, and turning on the light, I noticed the banging, now extremely loud, was coming from a radio. The radio, on the counter near the threshold of the back room, was off when I went to sleep! Wait, it was not even plugged in!

My pace quickened towards the radio until I was directly in front of it. The noise was altered, but still very loud. As soon as I picked up the radio, chills ran throughout my body and the sounds changed to a clear yelling voice, "*George, George, George!*"

I was not frightened when I heard my name being called from the radio or from the intense chills running through my body. I have no fear. I will say however, that I was absolutely surprised and startled to the highest degree. I immediately threw the radio down and ran, top speed, out of the shop. It was almost 5 a.m., but I called my mother's home in Staten Island to make sure Grandma Gerry was ok. I checked on Grandma Gerry to make sure it was not her who was calling my name. Her health was failing so I was concerned.

When Grandma Gerry arrived that morning I described the events to her. She quickly informed me that where I was standing in the work room, when I picked up the radio and heard my name being shouted, was the exact spot in which my *great-great grandmother Angelina* had suddenly died. Angelina is the same woman, spirit, that visited my mother three decades earlier.

Do your loved ones see you, hear you? Absolutely yes! This is another example of how connected we are with our loved ones who have passed, even family members we had never met before. There is a beautiful world where you go when you pass from this one. And your loved ones absolutely can and do see you, hear you, help you, and communicate with you! You are not alone! This life is not the end!

Of course, as I stated in Chapter 1, it is easier for you to communicate with your loved ones and your Guardian Angels when you are open to it. It is always much easier when there is no doubt or fear. When Grandma Gerry heard the voice warn her - she acted. Unfortunately, in the situation I just described with my great great grandmother Angelina, I ran out of the store not receiving her communication at that time. Sometime later, when visiting the Other Side, she was not available for direct communication, but in communicating with my Spirit Guides I was informed of why she came to me that evening. I was told that she wanted to get my attention to make me aware that things were about to change and not to let those changes interfere with my path.

My early experiences and continuous exposure to the supernatural have given me a unique perspective, understanding, and a knowing that, unfortunately, most people never receive. There are many individuals who, as children, may have experienced similar phenomena, but were discouraged by parents, adults, and/or peers. I have been experiencing and mastering the metaphysical since early childhood. Through hypnosis, I am able to unlock the infinite potential of my clients and students. Through hypnosis I am able to guide you to have similar experiences and attain similar abilities to explore, enjoy, create, and evolve.

One evening, at the age of six, sleeping soundly, I woke to my body tingling and vibrating. At first I was concerned because my body, tingling and vibrating, felt like it was frozen. It felt as though I was paralyzed! I was struggling to lift my immovable body up. Although I finally succeeded in rolling over, I fell to the ground. It was difficult for me to move, but I managed to raise my head and noticed my body was still asleep on the bed! I was no longer in my body!

Turning my head towards the door I noticed a beautiful bright light shining into my room from the hallway. Still unable to lift my energy body I crawled towards the light. As I was entering the light I felt a comforting warmth, a peacefulness, and joy. I lifted my head and was in awe to see Jesus standing in the threshold with arms half raised, as if to embrace me. It is very difficult to describe the feelings and emotions, but I did have energetic tears. They were tears of joy and love.

Jesus extended his right hand towards me. As I raised my hand to meet His, He lifted me up. We began to walk through the hallway towards the kitchen. We stopped in front of the refrigerator. He gestured for me to look inside as the door swung open. At first it was completely empty and then seemed to be over filled.

The dividing wall between the kitchen and the living room was not there. We stood at the edge of the kitchen where the wall was supposed to be for a long period of time. Where the living room was supposed to be was replaced by a vast emptiness. It was complete darkness, void of any light. The only light was that which continued to encompass us. Then I snapped back into my body.

It was an amazing and beautiful experience. When I was back in my body I felt such joy and peace. I was filled with immense gratitude, not only because Jesus came to me, but for all the great, and inexplicable, feelings. When I awoke the next morning I felt special. At six I felt so much clarity in my mind. I was excited to tell others of my experience.

My grandmother Gerry loved that I had this experience with Jesus. She would tell me that I was special and that I was blessed to have Jesus choose me to visit. My grandmother would remind me of my Jesus experience often. She had so much love for me and I felt her pride in me my whole life. Sharing the experience, with others, initially, was met mostly with, "that was a nice dream", which was better than the indifference displayed by my mother. No one understood that it was not a dream; so, I mostly kept it to myself. On occasion when I felt I could talk about the experience, it was met with a wide variety of subjective interpretation that hardly resonated with me. I did not understand the purpose of the visit, nor the message, for most of my life.

One explanation of part of the visit that resonated with me, or that I chose to resonate with me, was the explanation of the refrigerator. Many had said that the purpose of the refrigerator scene was that Jesus was letting me know that all I would ever need will be provided to me. They would say that there is infinite abundance available to me and to everyone who accepts Jesus into their life. Well, even at a young age I believed and accepted that there is infinite abundance available to everyone regardless of their belief or acceptance in Jesus. Although Jesus was bringing me important messages, the refrigerator being a small portion, I knew his message is to believe. He never said you had to believe in him. He said just believe. All you have to do is believe. Believe in yourself, believe in the infinite, believe you are eternal. Your very reality is shaped and absolutely created by what you believe. Whenever I need something it would appear or materialize in my life. I accepted that explanation and ran with it. Throughout my life whenever I need something it appears.

After that experience I remembered most of my astral travels very vividly. I would leave my body every night - at first just to fly, then to learn. When I did try to see Jesus again I was met with blocks or voices saying, "not yet". In my younger years, while traveling outside of my body, I would attempt to obtain the book of knowledge and to enter "Heaven". Again, before my teen years, I was stopped with a "not yet".

One evening, when I was approximately 14 years old, my energetic body and awareness began to exit my physical, sleeping, body with the usual tingling and vibrating. This time instead of being in my room I was instantly in an area with no seeming solidity. There was no floor that could be seen. There were no walls either. However, I was surrounded by various shades of purple mist. Where there should have been walls and a floor there were just flowing, shining purple mists of energy. Through the mist, before me appeared my great grandmother May, Grandma Gerry's mother, who had passed away about four years earlier. I thought to myself how much younger, and healthier, she looked than when she had departed.

As Grandma May greeted me she moved closer and began to speak. I felt a very warm, loving energy radiating from her to me. A complete peacefulness flowed through my awareness as I listened to her. She was assuring me that my life was going to be beautiful, my future was going to be amazing, that all I had to do was get through what I was experiencing in my current physical existence. Although, at that time in my life, I was being physically, mentally, verbally, and emotionally abused by my step-father every day, she promised me that my life was going to be great, that anything and everything was possible for me. Grandma May affectionately stated, as if I already knew, that I had important work to do. She urged me to continue being strong. As she hugged me, telling me that she loves me, I felt an enormous flow of peaceful energy, loving thoughts, and an optimistic attitude. When she stated to me that she had to go, I immediately returned to my physical body.

The next morning, visiting my grandparents in Brooklyn, I began telling Grandma Gerry about my last night's experience. As she listened it appeared as though her legs were weakening, she grabbed for a chair behind her and sat down. Her eyes watered as she explained that she had a similar "dream" with her mother last night as well. Grandma May came to her telling her that everything was going to be ok, just get through what she was experiencing right now. But the really interesting part of her experience was what Grandma May said to Grandma Gerry at the end, "OK Gerry I have to go now. I have to go see George."

Indeed, she did come to see me the same night. Coincidence? There could be many reasons that a psychologist might use to explain this away other than the beautiful, real, confirmation of life after death. One explanation, perhaps, would be that at the same time of this visitation Grandma Gerry and I were going through difficult times and our sub-conscious mind's defenses created, in our "dreams", a loving figure to comfort us and give us strength to endure. Perhaps. However, given the multitude of supernatural phenomena experienced by myself and my family it is easier for us to discount what a psychologist may say. If it had been our sub-conscious minds creating this visitation in our "dreams", why on an insignificant evening? Why only once and not repeated? Why and how did it occur the same exact evening? Again, Grandma May said to Grandma Gerry, before leaving her, "Ok Gerry I have to go now. I have to go see George". And she did! No coincidence!

Again, when you are open to the possibilities of communicating with your loved ones and your Spirit Guides you will receive signs and messages. When you know that there is life after death and you are open to it, and accept that communication is possible, it becomes even easier to do so. Your loved ones will appear to assist you along your path or help you and guide you in times of need. They do see you and are aware when you are going through difficult times. Especially when you are about to experience things in this life that you were not supposed to experience. During times of great despair, tragedies, or unnecessary discomfort they may show up, in various ways, to give you that needed strength. They will appear to give you a boost of encouragement, to let you know that you are not alone and that this life is temporary. All you have to do is just get through it.

If you refuse to accept it, at least, as a possibility you close the channels of communication. You may come up with excuses or other reasons as to what and why is being presented to you as signs, symbols, and messages from beyond. Unfortunately most people refuse to accept these possibilities because of fear - fear of being accused of being crazy, weird, strange, or abnormal. Most people will brush the attempts of communication from beyond away and ignore them completely. These people may believe they are preserving their sanity, but they are doing much more of a disservice to themselves and to their children. They purposely close these avenues to the infinite.

∞

In continuing to read this book my hope is for you to begin to open up to your natural born abilities to communicate with the positive and loving beings of the Other Side. Opening yourself up more and more to the truth of your eternal Soul you continue to expand and open those abilities to be receptive to the guidance and love from beyond this physical reality. By the time you reach the end of this book I am hopeful, even confident, that you will accept my invitation to visit the Other Side now!

CHAPTER 3: SOME OF MY METAPHYSICAL ABILITIES

"Anything and everything is absolutely possible with the power of your mind. Allow your mind to know that you are true infinite God energy"
- Geozuwa

"Only accept the positive because what you accept as the truth will be your reality"
- Geozuwa

To illustrate my perspective and perceptions it may be important to reveal some of my metaphysical abilities, at this point. Of course, just because I am able to experience and do what is seemingly impossible to the "normal" person, the metaphysical, does not lend absolute proof of the 'Other Side' and life after death. However, by discussing some of my abilities you will be more informed of where I am coming from and perhaps, more open to the possibilities of there being so much more to this physical reality than most people are taught, or what a "normal" person is supposed to believe.

Hopefully you will be more aware of why and how my, perhaps unique, perceptions were formed. I also want you to be aware that you too can have the same abilities. You do not have to have a near death experience or be zapped with gamma rays to have super human abilities. Although I have been doing the metaphysical, naturally, without being taught how to do the things that I do, I am passionate about unlocking all of these skills and abilities in the 'normal' person. I teach people all the time, through hypnosis, to develop and master metaphysical skills and abilities, and I love doing so! Perhaps, by sharing my reality with you will allow you to open up more to the infinite possibilities and your true eternal self.

I have been lucid dreaming since early childhood. Like most of my metaphysical abilities, as a child, I thought everyone was doing, and experiencing, the same things. When I began talking to my peers about my experiences, as though they knew by their own experiences, I was surprised and confused by their reactions. Not only were they confused by what I was telling them about my experiences, but they were starting to think I was crazy. So I decided to keep these experiences and abilities to myself and just enjoy my adventures.

Dream control has always been one of my favorite skills. I always absolutely love being aware that I am dreaming and then controlling the dream. As a child I mainly just flew. I would be dreaming and something in the dream would suddenly change, not make sense, and I would become aware that I was sleeping/dreaming. The moment I became aware that I was dreaming, I excitedly exclaimed to myself that I was dreaming and commanded myself to fly. Many times I would, where ever I was in the dream, start running and then jump into the air, flying over landscapes, mountains, buildings, the ocean, through the clouds and above. On some occasions, in the middle of a nightmare, perhaps being chased, I would become aware that I was dreaming and would quickly erase the threat, with the wave of a hand, or I would instantly begin to fly and allow the unpleasant dream to fade away.

Dream control sessions with clients are always so much fun. In the dream state we have unlimited access to the sub-conscious and unconscious minds. After guiding a client into a deep state of hypnosis I then guide the client into a natural sleep state while still being very aware of my voice. The client becomes aware that she is sleeping and dreaming. I then guide the client to correct, heal, change, and improve anything that she desires. I also teach my students to be able to control their dreams and fly every night. These skills are very effective when you want to turn a nightmare into a positive dream, or when you want to discover the answers to your questions. You can use lucid dreaming to study for a test, to master waking state skills, to prepare for any and all competitions. There are no limitations! And, for many, it is much easier to accept the absolute truth that there are no limits by developing dream control. For many it takes more of a leap to accept that there are no limitations in our everyday physical reality. However, for most people it is much easier, and readily accepted that there are, with absolute certainty, no limitations in the dream world. It is easier to accept that anything and everything is absolutely possible in your dreams. Therefore, through dream control hypnosis I can guide you to access all of your infinite potential in the vast and powerful sub-conscious, unconscious, and super conscious minds with absolute certainty and effectively create your perfect programming while having the most fun and enjoyment for yourself. Everyone loves to fly!

Flying in my dreams has always been so exhilarating! All of my senses are, completely awake to appreciate the freedom and joys of flying through the sky. A defining moment for my dream control skills and, unlimited possibilities, came about on a bus trip to Canada in my early teens. As my class stopped at a rest area, an article about lucid dreaming, in Omni Magazine, caught my attention. I have been doing it, naturally since infancy, and then I read about exercises and tips in the magazine to enhance the experiences. That first night after reading the article was amazing! I had the most vivid lucid dreams I had ever had up to that point. And following one of the tips, when control or awareness started fading in the dreams, I quickly remembered to spin to regain even more control!

The article also brought to my attention the fact that we can do so much more with lucid dreaming than just flying. It described certain ways in which you could solve problems, come up with solutions, and even heal yourself while dreaming. You can study for tests, learn new skills, recall memories, develop, practice, and train with new skills. I began a quest for knowledge and answers through my dreams. I trained in martial arts, sword fighting, and flying. I would create adventures for myself in the dreams with excitement and fun, which also granted me additional benefits and knowledge. Again, you too can easily develop and master these skills. I love teaching my students and clients this fun and exciting method of healing and learning!

To achieve many of my waking state desires I would go on magical adventures in my lucid dream states. For example, wanting a perfect memory, I created a magical world in my dream with unicorns, dragons, elves, and many other mythical creatures, in which I would go to accomplish certain goals. Before I fell asleep I would intend or declare what I was going to work on or achieve in the dream. Once I fell asleep and became aware that I was dreaming, I took control and flew to the magical world. In this adventure, I fought a dragon, rode a Unicorn, and overcame a labyrinth to find the magical memory potion presented to me by a powerful Elf Queen. I drank the elixir and felt the changes immediately. The next morning I awoke excited and grateful that I now had a perfect memory. From that moment on I have had a photographic memory!

Whenever I want to work on something specific, I usually drink a potion or a tea in the dream to achieve the desired results. At one point I was suffering with insomnia, mainly because my internal clock was out of whack, and it was interfering with my life. I decided to correct it in my dreams. I flew above the ocean, over the mountains, through the clouds, to a cave in the highest mountain above the clouds. When I entered the cave I was greeted by an elderly man in a robe with a long white beard. He waved his hand across the cave to reveal hundreds of cups and chalices. He instructed me to choose the right one and drink from it and I would be able to fall asleep whenever I wanted to, or needed to. After a few moments of careful consideration I drank the delicious and aromatic elixir and felt my by body warm and my mind tingle. From that moment on, not only did I never have insomnia again, but I could fall asleep anywhere, anytime, pretty much on command!

Several years before becoming a hypnotist I was in a serious relationship. I had very strong feelings for the woman. However, she just reached strike four. Since dating females I should have never dated, I have been as careful as possible in choosing with whom I would get serious. Usually, potentials would not get by the first strike. The relationship went beyond the point I should have broken it off. When a decision to end a relationship is made it is final. I do not play games. I do not answer the phone regardless of how much I may miss the person. If she were not the right person I would not give in. By the third day after the break-up I was feeling horrible. I was missing her and was almost giving in to calling her. She was not the right person for me so giving in was not an option. I decided to correct it in my dreams that night.

Before I went to sleep I told myself that when I was going to be off flying in my dreams I would drink a potion to eliminate all feelings for this woman. I also told myself that when I awake the next morning I would be completely amazed at how I would feel, and that I would have absolutely no feelings or thoughts of that woman. While lucid dreaming I flew to an old majestic building in the clouds. In the center of the grand room was a table with a filled cup. As I drank the contents I felt all of the effects immediately with gratitude.   When I awoke the next morning I was indeed amazed at how wonderful I felt.   I no longer had any feelings, whatsoever, for that woman.   I was happy and excited to move on with no negative thoughts or feelings at all.   I was completely free of any effects or residuals of that relationship. It was as though I had never been in any kind of relationship with the person.

These are just some examples of how I have effectively used dream control to correct issues in my life, while having fun and learning. You too can easily use dream control to heal, to learn, to expand your awareness, and to improve every aspect of your life. It is unfortunate that most are not aware that we have this ability and option to do amazing work with extraordinary results. Of course, just by sharing this ability with you I am hoping you are opening up more to the infinite possibilities.

∞

As a child I was fascinated with Superman's ability to see through walls with his x-ray vision. I was not quite aware, at a young age, however, that I always had a similar ability. During my earliest years I thought it was just my "imagination", but I was able to easily find hidden, lost, or misplaced objects. I could see, with compete clarity and details what was going on in a room on the other end of the house. I would see exactly where they were once the need arose.

Through most of my school years I thought I just had a photographic memory. Many times when taking a test, thinking it was my photographic memory, recalling the exact location in the text book, or my notebook, I would find the answer. However, there were many occasions in which I would see new pages or find the answers in different locations that I had never read before. For a time I thought, like any logical person, that I had to have been exposed to it on some level prior to the test. I just was not consciously aware of it. In high school, when taking an official timed practice SAT exam, I had searched for the correct answers in my usual fashion. I thought I would access my photographic memory to find the answers. In my search I was viewing the master copy with all of the answers. I had never been exposed to, or had any access to, the master copy prior to the practice exam. I still saw the answers very clearly and received a perfect score. The outside administrators of the practice exam and prep course were in amazement of my perfect score. When sharing this with Grandma Gerry she instructed me that if I do that I would not "really" be learning anything. She said it was "cheating". So for a long while when taking a test I would access only information to which I had been exposed.

I never knew, until someone explained to me in my early or mid-twenties that I was actually remote viewing. Once I became aware that that is what I was doing my remote viewing ability increased beyond all previous levels. Through the years I honed this skill to be extremely vivid from every angle, specific in time, through time, and outside of time. Of course, I mostly kept this ability to myself. Please keep in mind that I will never invade anyone's privacy whatsoever. I do not want anyone watching me or invading my privacy and I will, therefore, most definitely, not do it to anyone else. I am very ethical and morally guided by the Golden Rule.

∞

Sharing, sometimes with friends, they would say that it was great and that they wish they could do the same. They would always say, "You are able to know if your girlfriend goes where she says she is going to go, or doing what she told you she would be doing". Always, I would respond that if I thought that I was being lied to, or if I did not trust the person I was with, I just would no longer be dating the person. I would never invade anyone's privacy.

I, also, will never test it, to "prove" to anyone that I can do this. In the past, yes, I have shown and proven it. But.... well... I was dating a woman with whom I happened to confide in about some of my abilities. She was fascinated with the remote viewing. Everyday, from when I revealed some of my abilities, she asked me to "see" where she hid something. When I agreed to show her that I can remote view I specifically meant for it to only be one time. You can prove something is real or works a thousand times and then the one thousandth and one time, the only time, it does not work exactly how it should have most people will jump to say "it doesn't work".

So one day she comes into my office, closes the door, and asks me to find the object she hid in the house. I ask her if this will be the last time, as she assures me it is. I began to look like a high speed camera zooming through my house and in an instant I could see exactly where it was. I tell her it is in the second bedroom on the book, opened to page 37, with a T-shirt half covering it. Her expression as usual was, "OMG", with excitement as she grabbed me to show me that I was correct. That evening she came to me in my bedroom and said she did some things in front of the house and she wanted me to tell her by remote viewing everything in front of the house. With a sigh, I agreed to do it, even though she had said she would not be asking me to do so anymore, I had her reconfirm that she will never ask me again.

I described the location of every item, including a palm tree branch across the path, the two flower pots in switched locations, and a little white pebble on the doorstep. As soon as I mentioned the pebble she exclaimed that I was wrong and that was not where she placed it. I responded patiently, "That is what I see". She confirmed everything except the pebble. So we opened the front door and the pebble was exactly where I had said it was. Not only was the girl freaked out, but she was very frightened thinking I moved the pebble with my mind and wondering what other frightening things I could do. We stopped dating after that event.

That very evening as I was outside of my body, astral traveling, I heard a loud message, "Stop testing!" That message was shouted at me by one of my Spirit Guides. As stated earlier, communication with the Other Side and beyond is always available. I had accepted that message, or warning, and stopped testing my metaphysical abilities for others, as well as myself. I know how real all of this is, and there is absolutely no reason to test any of it. One of the reasons I teach my students to not test is because of the negating implications it can have. When one continues to test, especially after they have repeatedly confirmed the results, or the reality of the 'impossible', it leans towards a doubt. It is so very powerful, on every level, when you live in a state of knowing. You know what your given birth name is. You do not wake up every morning to test if your name is your name. There is no reason to. You know what it is with absolute certainty. When you transfer that same KNOWING to the infinite, to your Eternal reality, it is so peaceful, so fulfilling, and so very powerful. By the end of this book, hopefully, I will have taken you to a place of knowing. When you accept my invitation you will absolutely step into a beautiful world of KNOWING!

∞

I have been astral traveling since early childhood as well. In Chapter 2 I described one of my first consciously remembered out of body experiences involving Jesus. Many times growing up I would experience the same tingling, vibrating, "dream paralysis" feelings while sleeping. Instead of being fearful I always recognized it as the perfect opportunity to energetically leave my body with conscious awareness. To this day I always leave my body from the sleep state to do healing and spread Love and Light everywhere.

Many people, not knowing that I astral travel, not knowing that I do remote healing, have seen me at the foot of, the side of, or floating above, their bed during their night's sleep. They reported to me, that they were not sure if they were dreaming, or "This might sound crazy or weird, but I saw you last night with all of this bright light around you and there was this warm bright white light coming from you." And yes, when they would call to tell me this, although I usually did not tell them what I was doing for them, it was actual confirmation because I was indeed there doing exactly what they described.

On countless occasions when astral traveling, doing healing work, someone will pop up or appear that needs me. Many times people appear whom I have never met. I do not have to know who they are, what is wrong, or what they need. I am, however, confident that I give them exactly what they need when they need it. One day, while I was in Florida, around noon, I went into a deep trance, left my body, connected to Source, and went off to do healing work. I heard a calling out of despair and quickly went to where I was needed. There was a woman I had never met before crying with such sadness. I immediately filled her with Pure Love White Light, happiness, strength, courage, confidence, clarity of mind, clarity of purpose, and forgiveness. Her face began to smile. She was no longer sad and had a peaceful aura flowing all around her.

A few months later I was at a Yoga cafe in New York City. The very woman who I had never met approached me. She was smiling, but appeared to be a little nervous. She let me know that I might think that she was a little crazy, but she felt she had to tell me. The woman informed me that a few months ago in the middle of the day a great despair came over her. She felt as if she were at her darkest moment and just could not bear to live any longer. And she said at the very moment that she felt the darkest, the saddest, that she had ever felt, a warm beautiful light filled her and she could only see my face glowing directly in front of her. The woman, with a huge smile, explained that from that moment on she has felt better than she has ever felt in her entire life. She thanked me.

∞

I have programmed myself to be on auto-pilot and to go where I am needed the most when out doing my healing work. One night, as I was astral traveling, I was called to the sun. Yes our sun needed healing. I noticed several dark spots and black boxed shapes. I entered the sun, my energetic body vibrating and humming as I began to remove the black boxes. I was transmuting them to white light positive energy. I was filling the dark spots with Pure Love White Light directly from God through me.

I was interrupted abruptly and snapped back into my body from my wife shaking me to wake me up. She was concerned. She was woken up because my physical body was vibrating and she heard my body humming with a strange frequency. I told her there was nothing to worry about I was inside the sun removing black boxes and dark spots and I had to quickly return to finish. She was used to some of the physical manifestations of my body while I am astral traveling. On most nights I visit other worlds and other dimensions to bring Love, Light and healing energy to all. Sometimes, because the Pure Love energy is so unfamiliar to the beings of those worlds, they react aggressively, many times just out of fear, at first, attack me. Initially my wife was seriously concerned when I would snap back into my body in the middle of the night with very visible physical manifestations of those attacks. I always assured her that I would heal everything by the time we would awake in the morning. In the beginning she would take pictures of the manifestations in the middle of the night and was always delighted that everything was healed when we awoke.

While inside the sun, doing this healing work, I discovered that the dark spots and the black boxes were a form of cancer. This solar cancer was created by the negatives of the people of earth; the negative feelings, thoughts, intentions, and actions, such as the anger, the hatred, the guilt, the envy, the jealousy, the revenge, the hopelessness and much more. So I was filling the sun with love and forgiveness. And through the sun I was sending the inhabitants of earth forgiveness. Just as I do with clients in my office I brought the sun to heal with forgiveness.

I do not need confirmation of what I do. I know how real all of it is. However, I will receive confirmations none the less. The following day after sharing the events of what I was doing inside of the sun with my wife I went onto Facebook. Almost everyone's status feeds were filled with pictures of these brilliant auras around the sun, and filled with comments of how they had never seen the sun appearing the way that it was appearing that day. Everyone was in awe of how beautiful the sun shined that day.

When I teach others how to astral travel the first way in which they are programmed is to energetically leave their bodies from the natural sleep state. Many people report to me the same 'dream paralysis' experience. In most, there is an overwhelming fear because of their inability to move. They feel like they are awake, because their awareness is present, but they are actually already slightly out of their physical body. Being slightly out of the physical, not realizing it, they are attempting to move their physical body, they cannot and immediately they are struck with fear. However, that is a beautiful point to take control. Once they are aware that they are actually slightly out of the physical, with their intentions and no fear, they easily, and confidently leave their physical bodies and have amazing and beautiful experiences.

I, also, teach my students, whether in private sessions or in an Astral Travel Training Workshop, to energetically leave their physical bodies completely through self-hypnosis, and through each of their chakras. Each way in which you energetically leave your physical body to travel is completely different. Even leaving through different chakras will be vastly different. The feelings, the perceptions, and the awareness vary in great degrees.

In the Astral Traveling Workshops as students are leaving their bodies, most, actually see each other energetically outside of the physical. They wave to one another and smile, energetically. When I guide them to fly through the window, or walls, out into the city, they are energetically flying side by side. When they return they describe the experience and confirm who was together and what they experienced on the journey. Having the ability to powerfully and vividly see with my third eye I see each person outside of their physical bodies.

Before guiding students outside of the building I have them float around the room. Sometimes I will guide them to energetically float to the wind chime before I hit it. Some students begin to float to the wind chime at the opposite side of the room in which I am standing. At that point I will call out the names of the students floating to the other chime and have them float to the one near which I am standing. When they are all present I will hit the chime so they can feel, see, and experience something happening in the physical and differentiate all the senses while they are energetically outside of their physical bodies.

When they return from their travels, re-enter their physical bodies, and emerge from hypnosis they confirm all of their experiences. Not only do the students who were going to the wrong chime confirm that they were going to the wrong one, but the students who were already going to the right chime saw the students going to the wrong one before I mentioned their names.

You most likely already astral travel every evening without being consciously aware of it. I love to teach my students to astral travel on command in various ways with absolute awareness of the journeys. You too, if you are not already aware of it, can easily astral travel and be consciously aware. It is one of the many ways in which I guide my students to visit the Other Side.

CHAPTER 4: DOUBT

"Our doubts are traitors, and make us lose the good we oft might win, by fearing to attempt."
- William Shakespeare

"I shall not commit the fashionable stupidity of regarding everything I cannot explain as a fraud."
-
Carl Jung

"Question everything you are told to believe. No longer listen to what 'they' say. Change your belief system and allow yourself to be open to the infinite and eternal realities."
-Geozuwa

If you are like most people, you have experienced pain, hurt, loss, heartache, and various types of suffering. Some of you may ask why? Why me? Why would God allow such calamities to befall us? Many times through suffering it is easy to lose faith, questioning your existence and the purpose of it all. Although receiving knowledge and information from my relatives on the Other Side, from Spirit Guides, from Jesus, and directly from God, for a period of time I still had so much opposition to that belief system. Although now I am open and I know the reality of the Other Side, I did not always hold onto the certainty. I too had my doubts. There was a time when I was not absolutely certain about the Other Side or God. There was a time I was brushing aside possibilities and I was closing the doors to communication with my doubts.

Through my childhood I experienced severe abuse and torture at the hands and hatred of my stepfather from my 7th year until I left home near the end of my 16th year. My grandmother Gerry, very religious, would tell me the more you suffer on earth, the greater your reward in Heaven. She kept telling me that my mother loved my stepfather and she will still need him in her life when I leave home. She would tell me that once I turned 18 I could leave home and make a better life for myself. Grandma Gerry assured me that I was becoming stronger for my experiences. Regardless, it was painful!

With the help of my grandmother I always kept faith in God and Heaven. However, when I began Catholic high school my mindset and belief system began to change. One of the first lessons in religion class was that the Old Testament was not real. The Bible was just a bunch of made up stories inspired by God to teach lessons. But it was important to keep your faith. Looking back, and I do not mean to offend anyone, many of those lessons were horrible. Only men who have been manipulated and duped into not knowing their true infinite self can think that God would ever command his children to kill his other children. God would never command any people to conquer other people and take their women and children as slaves. Many of those lessons were to have unwavering faith and follow the "orders of God" because if you did not, you would suffer the wrath of God. You would be punished and perish at the hands of your enemies. But if you obey "God" you are rewarded with good fortune, wealth, and the destruction of your enemies. God would never command anyone to be put to death for not following his 'orders'.

The Holy Book, which I religiously followed all of my fourteen years of life, up to that point, was not real! The lessons Church and my grandmother taught me about faith and the power of God were based on fiction! This was a serious blow to me. I always had a personal relationship with God and always did the "right things". Faith was not enough!

I began to question and to logically deduce from my own physical experiences. I continued to be severely abused on many levels by my step-father. I was always doing the right things, being a good boy, doing as I was told by adults who were far less than moral. I saw, first hand, many priests as dishonest, abusive, and less than moral. The media coverage of priests sexually abusing young boys also put more doubt into me about the things they were teaching about morality, faith, God's will and so on. My grandfather had a few priest friends who had girlfriends and children. These priests drank, gambled, and engaged in immoral and illegal activities. At a young age, it became apparent to me how the church was only interested in money and power.

A quick note about the positive, and the usefulness, of religion: It may be necessary for individuals or groups of people, especially when going through tough times, to have a structured form of higher guidance or of a higher power to assist in daily living that may or may not be accurate. If, for the individual, the religion of choice is beneficial and provides a needed guidance that does not include control, manipulation, and forced ideology then it is good.   If the religious belief does not bring you to detest and hate people who do not believe exactly what your religion of choice is teaching you then it is ok.   If your religion of choice allows you to explore your true nature without any condemnation or negative judgment it is ok. If your religion makes you feel good about yourself, and the world around you, it is good.   If your religion guides you to think and act with love and kindness, for all, then it is good.   Of course, these are just my brief opinions.

Even though I continued to master Dream Control, Astral Traveling, and other metaphysical abilities, the physical world was really beating me up through high school and I was just so aware of the hypocrisy of "good and moral people". Also, science was trying to explain away my metaphysical experiences.   These scientific explanations and the false lessons of 'normal' people were throwing much doubt into my mind.   I just began to question everything that was taught. I did however continue to remain silent about my experiences and abilities. Even at this stage in my life, with certain people, I can never divulge a fraction of what I know and what I experience.

Several years ago I decided to reveal, just my dream control ability, with an older friend I had known for over a decade. When I described to her a little bit about what I do while asleep she became very concerned for me.   Why?   She felt I was escaping reality in an 'unhealthy' fashion, and I was not getting enough of a 'proper' sleep. She could not, or she refused to, comprehend what I was telling her. It just went against her perceptions of 'normal' and it made her react in a way that would allow her to keep her illusion alive by trying to convince me not to do it anymore. What was wrong with what I was doing? Shifting time in the dream state is so very easy. I could experience, and I teach my students to do the same, sometimes years of experience in only five minutes of actual sleep time. Five minutes do not interfere with a regular sleep schedule. Escaping? Some people use illicit drugs or drink in excess to escape with the most harmful effects on every level. I do not. Could going to a movie for two hours not be considered a form of escape from reality? Very rarely these days a movie is going to relay any benefits to you other than entertainment. Yes, I do enjoy going to the movies, when the movie is good. But five to fifteen minutes of lucid dreaming to learn, train, improve, heal, or just to fly, has more beneficial effects on your health and every other level of your being than a movie.

I valued my friendship with this person a great deal. A few years after I told her about dream control I decided to share with her about some of my other abilities including remote healing and going to the Other Side. Admittedly, I forgot about her reaction to the dream control. There was something going on in her life that prompted me to discuss this with her. I truly believed that she knew me enough to know that I was speaking from absolute clarity, never having any mental illness whatsoever. I presented her with countless testimonials of actual, real, everyday people experiencing miraculous healing from attending my workshops. She was not convinced! She was very, very, concerned! Thankfully, although this challenged all of her belief systems, she had enough sense not to try and commit me on the spot. Because of how I presented it to her she did step back and decided to contact a professional psychologist acquaintance of hers, who was open to the possibilities of metaphysical phenomena, to meet with me.

I was so sad and upset at the time, not only about my friend's reaction, but with her friend's limited perspectives. They agreed they could not understand, or accept for themselves, what I was sharing. Thankfully they also agreed that I was not 'crazy'! Her friend suggested I seek out others who could do what I do. However, that made me so much more careful about sharing information. At the time, I really thought that because I considered my friend to be intelligent, she would accept my offer to visit the Other Side. She chose not to because of her beliefs. Her religious belief did not permit her to experience God or the Angels firsthand.

∞

There comes a point in childhood when older children tell you there is no Santa Clause. Your parents tell you that is ridiculous, "of course there is a Santa, he brings you presents every Christmas, those children are not going to get presents, you have to 'believe' to receive gifts." So you continue to "believe" as other children are making fun of you, until you have had enough, and maybe your parents finally tell you the truth, "but don't tell your younger brothers or sisters, don't ruin it for them". I began to equate believing in God was the same as believing in Santa: an old man with a white beard judging, rewarding good behavior, and punishing bad behavior. It just seemed like a tool of belief to control people. As a child your belief in Santa was so strong, even when other children teased you that there was no such thing, you vehemently held your faith. Then it was all shattered as you matured and were "enlightened". Up until high school my belief in God was so strong, nothing could alter my faith, except for logic and "reality". If there is no Santa there is no God.

∞

In my early teen years, before I left home, I was really being hit hard from the world. One day, in the middle of a sunny afternoon, after being physically abused, an everyday event, my mother not caring, and the continued psychological torture I was enduring, combined with the constant physical signs and the "forced reality" of there being no God, "nothing 'Higher'", I truly despaired. I was in tears, emotional, I dropped to my knees, and I asked, shouting in my mind at God, "Do you exist?" That very instant, everything disappeared, I was in a black void of nothingness and a bright white light shined its warmth upon me from above. And from that White Light, a beautiful, strong, loving voice resonated, "YES!"

Then I was back in my room, still on my knees, in complete and utter awe. I remember thinking to myself, "what just happened?" It was the middle of the day, I was not asleep, and my eyes were still open. I was in a calm state of delightful confusion.

Looking back, with hindsight, that experience definitely helped me navigate my difficulties. I continued to enjoy my metaphysical experiences, keeping them to myself, but my path, during my teens, into my twenties, was an exploration of a physical mechanical world, with a scientific approach. One of my first classes in college, Psych 100, threw some curve balls at my beliefs. Hearing voices, ghosts, spirits, or other abnormal noises means you are mentally ill. Was I crazy? What about the experiences with family members happening at the same time? Psychologists would explain a shared experience as group psychosis with hallucinations of an auditory nature. So the dog would experience the psychosis as well? Unfortunately, most people will brush away certain auditory experiences because of a fear of being mentally ill. It would be so much more peaceful and beautiful to accept some of the auditory experiences as communication from beyond. Again, what would have happened if my grandmother was afraid of being 'crazy' when the voice told her that her children were in danger at the beach, when they were supposed to have been in school?

∞

Maybe I should clarify, at this time, without going into too much detail some of the cautionary signs. If you do hear voices of a negative nature, please do not listen to them. It does not necessarily mean that you are mentally ill, even if they are negative. However, it is possible that spirits of a less than positive nature can attempt communication. If any voice suggests you do anything of a negative nature please do not listen to it. The only thing that really means is that you must change certain things about yourself on certain levels. You must raise your frequencies and vibrations by doing positive things and or stopping anything you are doing that may be negative. For example, if you are abusing drugs and alcohol - stop. I understand most people are just operating on bad programming and cycles of dysfunction, but there comes a point to let go and end the cycles of dysfunction. If you are abusive, manipulative, controlling, vengeful, angry, or hurtful, please consider changing. Mainly, the only time less than positive communication could even be possible is when people are in weakened, negative, and serious self-destructive states. In all my workshops I make sure we eliminate all negative thought patterns, fears, the effects of trauma, abuse, guilt, shame and all other negatives. I love getting people out of their own way to improve every aspect of themselves, to enjoy life to the fullest, to walk along a higher path of Love, Light, and Happiness. I like to incorporate forgiveness therapies into my workshops as well as bringing a powerful awareness of always being protected. The Light is always more powerful than the dark. The higher your frequencies and vibrations rise, the higher more evolved entities are able to communicate with you.

∞

In college, at the time, most professors, learned, intelligent individuals, in my experience, were atheists. "Intellectual" students, as well, were just so against any "higher" powers. You were considered "enlightened" if you "knew" there was no God, no Heaven. It was just a mechanical world explained by science not by superstitions or magic. Like believing in Santa, it was ridiculous to believe in God. You were looked at as less than intelligent if you believed in the existence of God or a Heaven.

Regardless of my experiences and knowledge, I too was buying into the mechanical world. I was taking a strict scientific view of the world. Because of my metaphysical experiences and abilities I still knew there was much more to this physical reality than what is taught, or what most people believe. However, my logical mind was taking over my perceptions and viewpoints. Everything was random. There was no "Higher Authority" or "Divine Plan". We were on our own and everything came down to LUCK!

Luck, as defined by the Webster's College Dictionary, is the force that seems to operate for good or ill in a person's life, as in shaping events or opportunities. Luck determines the who, what, where, when, and how of everything. Luck determines every intention, every consequence, every judgment, and everything else that makes us who we are. This was one of the major premises of my senior thesis in college, in which I described the types of luck in a person's life, constitutive luck being the most important. I wrote that we do not get to choose what our genetic make-up will be. We do not choose what our physiological, and chemical make-up will be. We are born with it.

I even wrote that we do not actually have FREE WILL! Free will, as defined by the Webster's Dictionary, is the power or ability of the human mind to choose a course of action or make a decision without being subject to restraints imposed by antecedent causes, by necessity, or by determination. Our perceptions, our choices, and our way of thinking is shaped by our environment, circumstances, the people we come in contact with and every possible experience we have from birth until death. Even the nine months we spend in our mother's womb plays a great role in shaping what our will is going to be like. The developing baby will experience every thought, feeling, and emotion, the mother undergoes.

I wrote that it is a person's genetic nature, along with her physiochemical make-up, that processes all outside events, circumstances, and experiences. A person's physiological, and chemical make-up determines the way in which she perceives all of her experiences, the way in which she is affected or influenced by all of her experiences, and what she is able to learn from all of her experiences. It is a person's physiochemical make-up that makes her act and think, the way in which she does. Free will is just an illusion. Luck is governing and causing all of our thoughts, actions, and consequences.

My mechanical view during this time was very beneficial and actually helped me through tough situations. Granted, these were my earlier years, but, then, it took the mechanical view to understand the harm, and ridiculousness of judging.   People just could not get out of their own way. They could not see beyond their tortured lives.   They imprisoned themselves by being bound by their pasts, their experiences, and the negative conditioning of their environment.   To further complicate the human existence most people for some reason need to hold onto the limitations they create or allow society to create. They needed the suffering to define who they are.

The harshness of this world and the cards that life, seemingly random, deals us can push you to question it all.   Negative influences, situations, circumstances, and suffering can beat you into doubting anything higher. There came a time, in my scientific thinking, when I highly doubted what was taught, or what was commonly accepted religious interpretation. Because of my metaphysical abilities and experiences I did keep the possibility of the existence of Heaven open. I did, however, for some time, concentrate on the physical world. And I always questioned the sanity of what most people believed life was about. Most measured people success with income and wealth.

As an adult I was free from the abuse and torture of my childhood. The mechanical world view, combined with spiritual sense, allowed me to forgive easily. Holding onto anger, guilt, shame, and other negative thought patterns can only destroy you physically, mentally, emotionally, medically, and spiritually.   I knew at a young age of the power of forgiveness. You must forgive to free yourself to be happy, healthy, and enjoy life. Forgiveness heals everything!

∞

I have previously brushed over, by just mentioning, the abuse I experienced from my step-father. Regarding forgiveness now may be a good point in which to discuss some of that abuse. A few months before my mother was to wed my stepfather we were about to have a barbecue with many guests. My stepfather and I were setting up in the yard and something was forgotten. He was heading towards the front of the house when my mother appeared out of her bedroom window throwing me the item he was going to get. So I began calling his name so he would not waste the trip. My stepfather came storming into the yard, slapped me in my face and I fell to the ground. As I was on the ground he kicked me in the stomach knocking the wind out of me. Still having difficulty breathing he lifted me up by my throat. With his hands around my neck, I was choking with my feet barely touching the ground, he threatened me in a terrifying voice, "From now on you call me dad! If I find out you call me anything else but dad, even when I am not around I will break your fucking legs!" He then threw me back to the ground and yelled at me to get up.

I was seven years old at the time. I was petrified. He was not even married to my mother yet and I was forced to call him dad or I would be severely beaten. Pretty much the entire time I lived under the same roof with that person I was, not only beaten every day, more than once, but I endured mental and verbal torture. My brother always loved to play games to provoke my stepfather to punch or kick me, while he watched and laughed. Or he waited until after the beating and then he would tease me and laugh at me because he knew I couldn't do anything to him. For example, one night, while my mother was at work, my step-father, my brother, and I were having dinner. I do not remember their conversation while I sat there, but it came to my stepfather reaffirming to my brother that my brother could do whatever he wanted to do to me and I could not do anything to him. He told my brother to take his full glass of kool-aid and pour it on my head. My brother was laughing and said that I would get him later. My stepfather made me look at him with his cold stare of hatred as he commanded me with his harsh tone, "Your brother is going to pour his kool-aid on your head and you are going to sit there and take it. And you will not do anything to him. If I find out you do anything I will fucking beat you. He could do whatever he wants to you. If you do anything back to him I will make your life a living hell. You got it?"

My brother, with a big huge smile, walked over to me with his glass of kool-aid. Fighting back the tears, I was slightly shaking my head and pleading with him in my mind not to do it. He emptied the entire contents of his glass over the top of my head. As the kool-aid was running down my face they were both laughing. I had to clean up the mess right away, but I was not allowed to clean myself until I finished my meal, cleaned off the table, washed the dishes, and took out the trash.

It was my responsibility to clean the house, make everyone's bed, do the laundry, vacuum, mop, dust, clean the windows, do the dishes, the lawn, clean the bathroom, and everything else. I also had to make sure I woke up before my step-father every morning to make his coffee. Besides slapping me across the face or the back of my head without warning, he loved to punch me and kick me in the solar plexus to knock the wind out of me continuing to slap me while telling me to breathe. He occasionally enjoyed waiting for me at the top of the stairs. I knew I was about to be hit, and once I reached him at the top of the steps he would kick me so I would fall down the stairs.

Please keep in mind as you are reading this that I was a well behaved child. I did everything I was told to do. I was respectful and had good manners. I always did well in school. As a matter of fact my stepfather constantly put me down for being smart. He continued to try to make me be ashamed for being intelligent and bright, as though there were something wrong with me.

Where was my mother during all of this? For a time she would be working as he unleashed his battery of hatred upon me. She, as well as other family members, and friends witnessed more than enough of the abuse, but did nothing. On certain occasions I would get on my knees, crying, and begging my mother to do something. I pleaded with her that she did not have to leave him, but to please just stop him from hitting me. After I begged her, when she went to work, my stepfather beat me even harder calling me names and telling me that if I said anything to my mother again it would get a lot worse for me.   Many nights I cried myself to sleep and begged God to take me away, to just let me die. Many nights I prayed for death.

When I was thirteen, while we were on vacation in Florida, about to have dinner I sat there in a daze just being miserable after I had just set the table. With no warning I was struck in my face by the back of my stepfather's hand and I flew off of the chair.   As I picked the chair back up, holding back tears and being confused, my stepfather commanded me to say thank you to my brother. I said thank you to him not knowing why. Apparently my brother had given me an extra napkin. As I sat there, doing my best to hold back the tears, I just could not take it anymore. I turned towards my stepfather and politely made a request, "Dad", with a pause, "please don't ever hit me again."   With lightning speed, once I completed my request, he knocked me off of the chair with a punch to the face. He kicked me and started strangling me. My mother for the first, and only, time, tried to stop him. She jumped on his back screaming and as he tossed her off, I was able to break away from underneath. That was the only time, as well, that there was anything physical done towards my mother. I was not hit for a few days after that incident, but his campaign of abuse quickly returned.

I finally left home at sixteen years of age. I had no choice really. I was too old to be hit and it would come down to one of us being killed. I ran away, again, and was staying with friends for a few months.

The parents in the home where I was temporarily staying in wanted to charge my parents a monthly fee while I remained there. That was unacceptable for my mother. She did not want to have to pay anything. My mother was pleading with me to come home, promising that he would never hit me again. My stepfather caught me alone in the neighborhood, and with extreme hatred imparted to me, "I don't fucking like you. I never fucking liked you. You're not my son. The sight of you makes me sick. You disgust me. You can come back to live in the house because of your mother, but I do not want you there. It's my home and I don't want you there. I fucking hate everything about you".

So I have been on my own, supporting myself, since the age of sixteen. Of course, your mother is supposed to love you, nurture you, and most importantly protect you, especially when you are too young to protect yourself. Three years after I had already left home my mother told me that she was divorcing my stepfather. She explained to me that she never loved him and that she was only with him for financial security. She allowed a man to abuse and torture her son for a decade so she could have financial security.

Most people are operating on bad programming. It may take too long to go into details of my stepfather's and mother's past to illustrate how they were made to be the people they are. The important part is I forgave them. Yes the world can be horrible, heavy, and painful, but you must forgive. When you truly forgive you free yourself to heal on every level. When you forgive, you free yourself to enjoy life, and to be happy. When you forgive, you break the hold, and the control of what they, or the experiences, may have over you. For many, forgiveness may seem too difficult. But it is so important and powerful to forgive, to allow you to move forward in a positive and peaceful way.

∞

Keep in mind that the person, or the people, never have to know that you forgive them. You never have to speak to them ever again. The forgiveness is for you. Most people have the misconception that once you forgive a person you should go to lunch or dinner with them or have them over for tea. That is absolutely not necessary! Just because you forgive people does not mean that they change themselves. An abusive person will not necessarily change just because you forgave. When you forgive please remove yourself from abusive people and abusive situations. Just because you forgive does not mean that you should allow the person to continue to walk all over you. You never have to communicate with them ever again and in most cases it would be much healthier for you to no longer be associated with the parties who have wronged you, especially when it is of a very serious nature.

Most people are acting according to bad programming and allow themselves to be bound by the cycles of dysfunction. Most are not "lucky" enough to see beyond their situations and experiences to move forward with freedom and happiness. In the past my perception was that I was "lucky" to be intelligent enough to not allow my past to hold me down or hold me back in any way. I always wanted to help people, especially children. I always wanted to make a difference and provide alternate paths for children and young adults to escape the cycles of dysfunction and abuse. When I was young I felt I had to make a vast fortune first in order to help.

Forgiveness is one of our most powerful healing tools, but KNOWING that there is a Heaven, that death is not our end, and that there is much more to this life than what most people physically see and learn, can be just as valuable.

∞

As I was creating a real estate empire, building my fortune and wealth, it became more and more clear to me that it was not enough. There was an emptiness I could not fill. I have always wanted to help children, believing I needed to build a vast fortune first. But how much was enough? Then it seemed as though things were happening to push me in a certain direction. I was guided by forces from beyond this physical reality to study and train in hypnosis.

Let's address the doubts that you may have. I revealed a little bit about my experience with this heavy world and how it could beat a person into doubt. Some people absolutely refuse to hear or read anything that slightly varies from what their personal religion tells them to believe. Religion could put so much doubt into a person's mind for many reasons on many levels. It is funny how they want you to believe in a life after death, but they do not want you to access it or experience it until you depart this world. Could it be they do not want you to know the truth? You might find out that you do not have to kill people who do not believe in your version of God and Heaven. You might find out that the only person who judges you is you.

You might find out that mostly everything you were taught and were told to believe in is false. Yes, for some people that can be very scary. People do fear the truth. People fear the unknown. People fear change. Sometimes it takes real courage to objectively look outside of yourself and examine what you have been lead to believe.

I too experience the heaviness of this world. There was a time in my past I too brushed aside the magnificent beauty of the Other Side; perhaps because I allowed the world and my circumstances to get the better of me. Maybe I rebelled against the Infinite Truth because I was hurt. Thankfully my Guides, my Angels, my Soul's family, and the Infinite Pure Love Energy did not give up on me.

There are infinite possibilities of the why's and why nots. Maybe you are reading this book now because your Guides are not giving up on you and want you to awaken to the Infinite. Perhaps, with immense gratitude, they will continue to guide you to accept my invitation to experience the bliss and beauty of the Other Side now, to accept your true infinite and eternal self. Your Guides do want you to consciously be aware of them and most importantly they want you to be aware of yourself. If you already do communicate with your Guides it will be my pleasure to direct you even higher along your path. After reading this book you may be eager and excited to meet them face to face.

CHAPTER 5: SIGNS - WAKING UP AGAIN

"We are travelers on a cosmic journey, stardust, swirling and dancing in the eddies and whirlpools of infinity. Life is eternal. We have stopped for a moment to encounter each other, to meet, to love, to share. This is a precious moment. It is a little parenthesis in eternity."
                                                              –Deepak Chopra

"You are a beautiful, amazing, and powerful being of Love and Light. Awaken to your true infinite and eternal self."
                                                              -Geozuwa

How many experiences, or at least, how many stories have you heard of about people "luckily" or "coincidentally" diverting catastrophes or even cheating death?   Have you heard the stories of the people working in the World Trade Center in New York City who never took a day off, not even a sick day, from work in ten or twenty years, who for "whatever" reason called in sick the morning of 9/11?   I personally know a few of those individuals.   And I personally know many who have had similar experiences, including myself and family members. Were these experiences just luck or coincidence?

I now know with absolute certainty there is no such thing as luck or coincidences.   Everything that happens or does not happen is a direct result of what we create, co-create, and choose.   How I am so certain will be discussed in greater detail later on.

This chapter is about the signs, the "coincidences", that woke me up again and allowed me to embrace who I am and who you are. We are Eternal and powerful beings!

First I will discuss the meaning behind signs and "premonitions". When an object moves, or something falls off of a table or counter with no apparent reason, these are some of the signs you may have, or will receive, from time to time. Perhaps the doorbell will be ringing, or there will be a knocking on the door, with no physical explanation. Perhaps objects are moved or rearranged. Maybe, certain animals would appear, out of the ordinary, knock on your door, or the animals just made sure you noticed them. These are signs or messages.

In doing the metaphysical and in communicating with Spirit-Guides, or Guardian Angels, I have learned that, often, the meaning of the paranormal signs is just to let us know that we are not alone. Spirit-Guides and loved ones, especially in times of need, will let us know they are there for us. Another reason they communicate is to let us know that there is so much more to this world, to our lives, than what we physically experience and what we are taught. One of the main messages is that there is life after death.

One of my great grandmothers was nearing the end of her life. Although she was admitted to the hospital, I remember my mother was very hopeful that she had more time left. A couple of days after she was admitted to the hospital I was playing with my younger brother in his bedroom. The window with a screen was open. We were startled and froze when a crow crashed into the screen. The screen fell into the room and the crow stood there and cawed for a few seconds inside of the bedroom. As soon as the crow flew away I called my Grandma Gerry, but she asked me not to tell my mother. She explained that when a bird flies into your home it means someone in the family is going to die. Well, my younger brother told my mother as soon as she returned home. She cried hysterically for at least an hour. My great grandmother passed away a few days later.

In my family, for many years, various birds delivered the message that someone in the family, or a close friend, was about to die. This type of message, with birds flying into my home as a child, and as an adult, took place before all of my great-grandparents, all of my grandparents, cousins, friends, and other closely associated people had passed away. Nowadays, however, I no longer receive these messages before someone dies. A person, a friend or a relative, will energetically say good bye to me before they pass or their soul stops by and engages me before they move on, after they have passed away. Many times a person will appear to me, while I am astral traveling, for guidance, forgiveness, and to heal their friends or family members they are leaving behind. After the visit I would discover that the individual has just passed away.

When I began the drafting phase of this book my neighbor from childhood, Cynthia, visited me three nights in a row. I had not seen her or spoken to her in almost twenty years. The three nights she came to visit we discussed what her life would be like if she made different choices at certain points in her life. I kept assuring her that everything she did and all of her choices were ok. On the third night as she was saying goodbye, behind her smile, there was still a deep sadness of regret and pain that came to my awareness. At that very moment I had her stop. I directed Pure Love White Light Healing energy from the Source of all creation through me to her. As I was filling Cynthia with this energy I was directing absolute forgiveness to her. With my many pure positive intentions, as I was healing her with absolute forgiveness, I also freed her from any and all aspects of negative karma. At that moment she was completely free of any karmic contracts and obligations from this life and any of her other lives. I found out a couple of days after her last visit that she had just passed.

∞

Many times as I am astral traveling people will come to me or call me for assistance and or healing. I will speak of this in more detail later on in the book. However, I am sharing some of this right now as it relates to people visiting me or calling me, energetically, before leaving this physical world. Sometimes when someone is calling me they are at a critical point in their lives. Other times a person is faced with the decision of allowing their life to end, I find out later that they were in the hospital in critical condition, and to move on and they needed guidance. If they decide it is time to go I share Pure Love and absolute forgiveness with them.   However, many times a person I may have known in the past will visit, not because they are dying or have just passed away, but because they just need a boost of energy from Source. When I direct this Pure Love energy to them I combine it with my pure positive intentions of strength, courage, confidence, clarity of mind, clarity of purpose, perfect health, perfect vision, peace, happiness, and forgiveness.

Interestingly, as I was finalizing this book before publishing, a friend from junior high school visited me. I probably had not spoken to him in over twenty years. During his visit we were laughing about all of the fun we had in school. He said, "I really want an eighth grade reunion before I leave".   Another junior high friend, Gina, came to my awareness who always wanted an eighth grade reunion, but departed this world very young.   However, I did not have an awareness that he was about to pass away. So when I awoke the next morning I had connected to Source and sent him Pure Love energy with all of my pure positive intentions, combined with forgiveness, for him and his family.

One day later as I logged on to Facebook the first post I see is from another good friend from junior high that Rob had just passed away the day before. Within one day of the news of his passing an eighth grade reunion was organized. I am sure that Rob and Gina will be present.   I am also sure that they will make their presence known and felt.

∞

Various birds will come to me now to relay specific messages of a different nature. Sometimes a duck, a cardinal, a woodpecker, or a vulture, will come to give me messages. Many times hawks will land in front of my home's door; sometimes a hawk will land on the roof of my truck as I am walking towards it. Many hawks happen to perform other signs to relay information to me; for instance, on occasion a hawk would swoop in front of me, within a couple of feet, before an incident, and after the incident, to remind me of who I am, and not to allow the incident, regardless of how upsetting, influence me, or push me into a less than divine response, or lower path. The hawk and eagle are my main messengers. My Soul Mate's bird is the owl. Before meeting her in this physical reality her owls have looked out for me and warned me in certain situations to prevent me from making mistakes. An owl would crash, unfortunately, into my windshield, sometimes just missing my windshield, to really get my attention, to warn me, and prevent me from making wrong decisions.

Ted Andrews has written books describing the meanings of when certain animals come into your life or cross your path to give you messages. That may be a good guide for beginners to receive messages from their Spirit Guides. However, none of what is written is necessarily true. When Spirit Guides need to relay information to us, sometimes, they will enter, or at least guide, an animal to deliver that information. There are infinite possibilities of what something may or may not mean. I believed, as a child, that any bird flying into my home was a sign that someone close was going to die. When it happened someone passed away; sometimes the family member or friend who passed away was a complete surprise to everyone. The surprising ones even included young people passing away. Most signs received from above are just messages that you are not alone. The beautiful part about being who you are is that you can make any sign or message mean anything you want it to mean and it will mean exactly that!

If you choose to believe a message means what someone else tells you it will mean exactly that. It is important for you to know that you are an absolute creator. As you continue your learning journey please do not accept any teaching from anyone that incorporates limitations or negatives. The only limitations you have are the ones you place on yourself or the ones you allow others to place on you. You are truly an eternal Soul with infinite possibilities. So please only accept the positive because what you accept as the truth will be your reality.

∞

I was always interested in hypnosis and the power of the mind from early childhood. There were times I would look for hypnosis schools with no success. My mechanical wealth seeking journey brought me to invest in Florida real estate and then to become a licensed builder. All of my investments, then my building projects, were near my mother's house in Florida. Interestingly, when it came time to buy my own house in Florida instead of traveling from New York City to conduct business, I bought a house almost two hours away from my empire. Why?

Before I moved to Florida I had recurring dreams of helping people through hypnosis. Almost on a nightly basis I had dreams of teaching large groups of children hypnosis. And in these dreams I watched them grow into happy and healthy adults filled with love.

Well, every day on my way to my properties and building sites I drove by the Omni Hypnosis Training Center. Once I noticed it, I knew that one day I would take time to become a certified hypnotist. I did not want to do it for a job or a career. I wanted to use it when I was financially where I thought I needed to be to help children and others. I, also, wanted to explore hypnosis to increase and improve my metaphysical skills and abilities, and to enhance my mind's power.

The owner and hypnosis instructor of the training center was Gerald Kein. Discussing past life regressions and the confirming information received from previous lives of Jerry's clients began to open my eyes again. The state of life between lives is amazing! Most of us do choose our parents, our lives, our paths, the difficulties and our experiences! Luck has nothing to do with it! The various metaphysical hypnosis techniques and sessions will be discussed in the next chapter in detail. I just want you to be aware that when I finally did the hypnosis course signs started to occur in abundance.

In twenty something years of my life I had never run over anything; however, as I was driving near my properties one day, a cat ran out, seemingly deliberate, directly under my truck. The following evening as I was driving in an area with more traffic a dog, seemingly deliberate, as if it specifically chose my truck, ran under it. I pulled over, but the dog was gone. The next day the same thing happened with a raccoon. In my whole life this had never happened, then suddenly, three animals in three days. It felt like what was happening was out of the ordinary. I thought about it for a few days trying to discover its meaning. I mentioned it to friends, who quickly explained it as coincidence. Yet it felt like so much more than coincidence!

The day I decided that it definitely did not feel like coincidence something else took place. That very evening, as I left my body, directly in front of me was an amazingly beautiful woman! Her hair was a subtle reddish gold, her skin was a radiant milky alabaster, and she was dressed in a flowing white and silvery gown. There was a shimmering glowing light all about her as she just smiled the warmest smile I had ever experienced. I did not try to do anything. I was not even thinking. I was just enjoying the experience.

The next day as I drove, the weirdest things began to happen. At different points in the day three different animals would run to the road, stop suddenly, and wait for me to pass. The same thing happened for nine consecutive days, with three different animals each day including, dogs, cats, raccoons, squirrels, coyote/fox, rabbit, turtle, and opossum. These events were definitely not coincidences, but what did it mean?

Around the same time my youngest brother was staying at my house for a week. We would go for walks and talk. While we were walking one of those days, a car, filled with teenagers, on the opposite side of the road beeped at us, when we looked everyone in the vehicle gave us the middle finger. My brother asked me what I did, but I had not done anything. Within five to ten minutes a car with two adults slowed down near us walking to make sure we noticed them giving us the middle finger. We were both very surprised. We checked to make sure we did not have any signs on our backs to provoke random people from giving us the middle finger. It happened a few more times during our walk and not to anyone else who was walking around. We were discussing it and laughing about how none of it made any sense. The last car of our walk slowed down to reveal two elderly women, who seemed as though they could barely see over the dash board nor through their thick spectacles, they did not smile, nor say anything - they just looked at us and they both gave us the middle finger, and drove off.

There are infinite possibilities as to what these signs or messages were. Now, if the meaning behind such occurrences did not instantly come to my awareness, I would bring my mind to the higher states of awareness to receive the message, or I would astral travel to discover the meaning, or I would use any one of the many other retrieval techniques. When these incidents took place, I knew they were directed at me to get my attention. I knew, without connecting to Source, they were messages for me to stop ignoring the infinite. We are not alone. They were getting my attention to stop ignoring their signs and guidance. I needed to get back to doing my healing work.

Those simple occurrences were more than enough to re-ignite my true self. I did not wait to consult with anyone any further. Usually when consulting so called "enlightened" or "spiritual" teachers I was amazed at how limited they are and I was disappointed in their lack of true knowledge or wisdom. I am not saying I am better or that I know everything, but I do know that there are infinite possibilities. I do know that we are eternal beings with infinite energy and powerful abilities to create. So, I began, with full force, to continue doing my remote healing. Every night before sleep, while I slept, and astral travelled, every morning when I awoke, and any chance I could get throughout the day I astral traveled. The world was changing or rather my vision and perceptions were changing. I was waking up again! My awareness on every level was increasing exponentially! And I noticed all of the healing and metaphysical work I was doing resulted in what many would consider miracles!

Confiding with friends about some of the healing was met with laughter, or accusations of being crazy, or politely being told they were coincidences. Having heard enough rationalizations and jokes, I decided to keep it all to myself. But I did want to test, again. And I say again because as a child I always tested and was always met with solid confirmations of how real and how easy the "impossible" was. Growing up I would astral travel to people I hardly knew and give them messages to give back to me and they did. Many times they did not know why they were doing the things they were doing or relaying messages to me - it made no sense to them. Sometimes they were very interested in the metaphysical and I was able to divulge certain aspects of my adventures. Sometimes what was revealed seemed too powerful or overwhelming. There were times when a person would be really interested in lucid dreaming and astral traveling, and practically beg me to visit them, even enter their dreams. And yes, these instances of dream sharing and astral visits, were confirmed with written and sealed accounts of the experiences from myself and the other parties. Unfortunately, after confirming how real these experiences were, it created more fear in the individual and in the friends with whom they happened to trust the information with. Even with all of their interest and curiosity, once the reality was revealed to them, they were, unfortunately, filled with much fear. Many choose to fear what goes against their initial worldly perceptions and beliefs of what they think the world is, or what they have been taught the world is supposed to be.

∞

One morning, awakening around 5 a.m., I decided to perform a test. I put myself in a trance, energetically left my body, and went to my mother's home. She was still asleep. With my energetic body next to her bed, I began to fill her with healing white light at the same time I was repeating to her, "Today is going to be one of the best days of your life, you are going to be the happiest you have ever been in your entire life, and you are going to be really surprised if anyone asks you, because it is one of the greatest days of your life, you are the happiest you have ever been and you do not even know why."

When I was finished, I returned to my physical body and then left to work for the day at my building sites. I stopped at my mother's house at the end of the day. As I was sitting next to her, about to watch "Law & Order", I asked, "Hey Ma, how was your day?" She looked at me with the biggest smile and said, "Today was the greatest day of my life, I was the happiest I have ever been". She leaned in closer to me, "And I don't even know why".

I know how real all of this is. Although I no longer look for confirmations I continue to receive them in abundance. My goal is for you to wake up as well. Perhaps you are already awake and this is another step in the waking process. We are all on different levels. And that is okay. My goal is to guide you to evolve your Soul to the highest levels. To assist you in expanding your awareness to levels you may have never dreamed possible. One of the first steps is to acknowledge that there is life after death. Become aware and accept with certainty that your Soul is eternal. Perhaps as you are reading this, whether you are aware, or not, of the perfect place from where you have originated and to where you are returning when this brief journey of physical life ends, you are becoming more open to visiting the Other Side now.

∞

My intentions are pure. There is absolutely nothing I want from you except for you to be aware of your true infinite self. I want you to be the perfect you, to enjoy life to the fullest. I want you to know that you no longer have to suffer with anything ever again. I want you to live your perfect life of infinite abundance, of happiness and joy! Discover it all for yourself. Be the amazing and powerful creator you were born to be! I do look forward to seeing the beautiful world you co-create with all of our evolving Souls. Thank you for being you and for continuing your journey and learning experience in a positive way.

CHAPTER 6: METAPHYSICAL HYPNOSIS

"Holding on to anger is like drinking poison expecting the other person to die."

-
-Buddha

"Forgiveness is one of our most powerful healing tools. When you forgive you free yourself to be the perfect you. Forgiveness frees you to live your perfect life of infinite abundance, of happiness and joy with perfect health"

- Geozuwa

Before I officially became certified as a hypnotist through the National Guild of Hypnotists I completed an at home certification course. I started my journey as a hypnotist, not for a career, nor for an income, but to help people and perhaps to expand my metaphysical abilities. With hypnosis I was able to get people out of their own way to truly change and be happy.

One technique to help clients is to regress them to the cause of the problem of why they have sought my services. Sometimes the client would regress to a previous life. I believe the statistic is three out of ten clients will regress to a previous life because the issues they are experiencing in this life were carried into this life from a previous life. Many of the issues were unresolved and they needed to be addressed.

Many times when a client becomes aware that their issues were carried forward from a previous life it is more than enough to let them go. However, the most important factor in permanently eliminating the issue is for the client to forgive; not only forgiveness, in the past life, of all involved and the previous self, but forgiveness of all players in this life who may have contributed to the issue's existence. The client must also forgive herself in order to be absolutely free of the issues - forgiving self for bringing it forward into this life and forgiving self for allowing it to effect the client in the way it has. Then the client must forgive herself of any and all infractions towards others and self whether intentional or unintentional. Forgiveness is crucial for the success of this therapy and for the client to move forward without being effected by the causes and the effects of the initial event. Forgiveness is one of our most powerful healing tools.

∞

When doing real past life regressions the clients' previous lives, many times, are very boring. Some are housewives doing dishes as their children are playing at their feet. Most are ordinary people having ordinary experiences in the early 1900's, 1800's, 1600's, and well into the distant past. Some were Nazi soldiers, some were Jewish prisoners at concentration camps, some were farmers - variations of every occupation and level of society.

One woman who came to see me to correct her breathing issues, when regressed to the initial sensitizing event (ISE), she went back to an incident two lifetimes ago. She was a little girl on a crowded boat sailing from South America to the U.S. It was on fire and she died with everyone else at sea. During the life right before the present, she survived for a few weeks and then died of breathing complications. Once the woman realized the issue was from previous lives she became more confident she could eliminate the problem in this life. After we did the forgiveness she was completely healed!

While she was guided through her past lives and then into this life we discovered that in this life she was born to the son of the woman who gave birth to her in that short physical existence she experienced. The woman, informed me upon being emerged from hypnosis, that she had the strongest connection and bond in this life to her grandmother, the woman who had given birth to her in a past life. She also informed me that she thought her grandmother only had one child, her father. A few weeks after our session she reported to me, after speaking with her mother, that her grandmother had, in fact, given birth to a daughter who only survived a short while.

∞

In teaching my National Hypnosis Certification Course I make sure every student is apt at doing regressions. In the training, however, I have them practice regressing classmates back to happy moments in each life. This gives them the ability and the confidence to perform the therapeutic regression sessions when they begin their own practice.

When people are truly regressed they are not just remembering the events, but it is as though they are actually there, reliving the experiences. The client mainly speaks in the present tense and describes the self as the person they are in that particular life. A woman can be a man in a previous life, and vice versa. In taking one woman back to happy moments in past lives, she was a man on his farm in Germany milking a cow. That was the happiest moment? I asked 'him' if he were married. A negative response was accompanied by a fading smiling. I asked if 'he' had a girlfriend. This negative response was accompanied by much sadness. Since I was being filmed on a television program, and it was only supposed to be happy moments, I allowed the woman to have the scene fade and brought her/'him' to a happy moment at a much younger age in that life then brought her to other past lives. In some lives she was learning how to swim at the beach at four years old. She was eleven years old in another life at a music school learning how to perform.

∞

What does past life regression prove? It most likely adds to the evidence that your Soul lives and continues to be reborn through thousands of lifetimes. Maybe. As always there are infinite possibilities. When I was training with Gerald Kein he told a story of doing a past life regression that turned out to be something more. I will relay that story to you now.

An older Italian American man, with an accent, came into Gerry's office pleading with Gerry to please help him, and fix his neck. The man was born unable to move his neck from side to side. He tried everything from doctors, chiropractors - you name it he tried it. Now he wanted to give hypnosis a try.

Gerry placed him into a deep state of hypnosis and regressed him to the cause of why he had this neck condition. When the man arrived at the cause his face was smiling and he said, with a chipper voice and an Irish accent, "Hello, top a the mornin."

Gerry started doing the routine when you first regress someone, "Is it day time or nighttime?"

"It's the wee of the mornin. A lovely mornin." The man's response was with a tone of an energetic happiness.

"Are you indoors or outdoors?", Gerry continued to ask.

"I'm outdoors, man.", he answered with a tone implying that these questions were ridiculous.

"Are you alone or are you with others?"

"I don't know what is wrong with you. If you are just blind or dumb. But the whole town is here, can't you see?", the man responded as though Gerry was there with him and should be aware of everything that was happening.

"You'll have to forgive me I'm not that bright, so can you tell me what is going on?", Gerry stated and asked so the regressed man would not continue to get more irritated.

"They're about to hang me.", the man responded sounding apologetically for insulting Gerry, then quickly returning to his happy go lucky regressed self.

"Why are they going to hang you?"

"They're hangin me for being a horse thief", the man replied with a big smile and a happy go lucky voice.

Then with more of a whispering voice, "But that's not the real reason they're hangin me. No. Everyone in the village is a horse thief. I'm a really fine lookin lad and I have a way with women. So, when the men of the village go off to work I go to work on their wives."

Gerry brought the man through the hanging, his death, and to a state after death, before this life. If my memory serves me, this was the first time Gerry experienced this type of session. After the hanging the man's physical appearance, the smile, changed. The man lost his accent, both of them, and was speaking with a soft mono-tone now.

The man described to Gerry where he was, answering many questions about this life between lives, mostly stating "you wouldn't understand yet". The Soul does not die. The physical body and the brief physical life on earth is a drop in the bucket for our eternal Souls.

The man stated that you are not judged by anyone else. You judge yourself. When you depart the life on earth, you review your previous life. In reviewing his previous life he felt that he had to be reborn again and compensate for the mistakes he made in his previous life. This person who was now "living a life" between lives explained to Gerry that in his previous incarnation he was so charming and charismatic. He could have done so many wonderful things and he could have really helped others. Instead, he used his charm and charisma in a negative fashion for selfish and carnal desires and needs. He destroyed so many families and lives as a result of what he did. His actions and misdeeds caused a great deal of sadness and pain in many people. So he decided he needed to suffer in the next life.

Just a quick side note: If the man living in the Irish life had truly forgiven himself before he left that life he would not have brought that issue forward. His Soul would have recognized that his physical existence realized what he had done and the suffering he caused. Perhaps there would have been no reason to carry it forward because the lesson had been learned and understood. I write perhaps because, again, it is up to the individual. Maybe the man's Soul could have thought that it was not enough.

Gerry would not stand for it. He immediately reprimanded the man between lives by telling him that he was being selfish and ridiculous. Gerry explained to him that the man who is living this current life sitting in the office has suffered enough. He was born that way and suffered for over fifty years and that it was not fair to hold onto it any further. After a period of a back and forth Gerry convinced him, the life-between-lives him, that he has suffered more than enough for the indiscretions and mistakes of the previous life, and that it was time to let go and give the current incarnation a chance at happiness, free form the neck condition. After all of the forgiveness work in the previous life, the life between the lives, and the current life he emerged the client.

The client with an expression of complete awe, along with his Italian accent asked, "Gerry, was that real?"

Gerry, "You tell me, you were there."

"But Gerry, I was a neva Irish."

The gentleman came to visit Gerry a few times after the session. Each visit he showed Gerry he had more motion in his head and neck. A few months afterwards the gentleman showed up with his whole family and a bunch of baked goods, everyone thanking him, as the gentleman showed Gerry that he had nearly 100% neck mobility.

My clients and I love doing these sessions. I, often, will do past life regressions, lives between lives, and then future life progressions in combination, depending on what the client's needs are. There is a great value in doing these types of sessions because the client becomes aware of certain aspects of their life's path. You learn what lessons you have chosen to learn in each life and if you have accomplished the goals you have set out for yourself.

∞

When doing future life progressions the results are pretty much the same. Ordinary people living ordinary lives. In some of the futures, names of countries have changed, along with big climate changes. In doing future life progressions with some clients we discover that they are going to have several, sometimes an indefinite large amount, of future lives here on Earth. However, the same clients, after attending my 2-Day Healing Workshop & Evolve Your Soul Training, discover that their future lives on Earth drop down to one or two, but most discover that this is now their last physical life on Earth.

Each client regardless of their belief system, religious or not, have these lives between lives in which they inhabit the Other Side. They confirm a beautiful, peaceful place, with no ego, with higher loving energy. Any sceptic, with their worldly experiences and events, will say, "It's just in the client's mind", even after reading about a plethora of hypnosis clients' experiences. They may stay in a state of disbelief and continue to say, "It's just their imagination". And that is ok. I still have a lot more to impart to you.

You may have read books about past lives, there are several, in which they give 'definitive' descriptions of certain time periods, even those of Atlantis. It must be noted that there are infinite possibilities. A hypnotist could have several clients, unrelated, come to her office for past life sessions, and it is discovered they all knew each other or were there around the same period in those lifetimes. There are no coincidences. There may be reasons though, why the clients, and the hypnotist needed to experience these sessions when they did. It is extremely irresponsible to claim an entire civilization to be exactly how one individual describes it, even if several individuals have the same descriptions. Imagine a thousand years from now someone is regressed to today's world. And the regressed individual is a member of an indigenous tribe of the Amazon who, yes they are still out there, has never had contact with our 'civilization' or anyone outside of their tribe. How would that person describe this world? There are so many cultures on this planet alive today, with countless sub-cultures, even subs of the subs of sub-cultures. With approximately seven billion people on this planet - each person has a different idea of this world - each have their own reality. How would a police officer in New York City describe his world? How would an anti-government type, with all of the 'conspiracy' theories, describe this world? How would an actor or politician describe this world and the people in it? How would a racist, believing there is a race war always imminent, describe this world? How would a teenager in the foster care system, who experienced severe abuse at the hands of the people who are supposed to protect, love, and nurture her, describe this world? How would religious, of any religion at all, fanatics describe this world? I could go on, and on, and on. So please be aware that there are infinite possibilities. No world, our world and time included, could have any single description to give justice to our infinite diversity.

∞

One of my most favorite sessions to do with clients is to bring the client's current awareness to the Other Side. Yes, the Other Side! I take you to the deepest states of hypnosis, separate your mind from your body, and then guide your mind, free of the physical restraints, to the higher states of awareness. When I bring you there, you are face to face with loved ones who have passed, if they are available. Face to face with your Spirit Guides, Guardian Angels. You receive valuable information about your life, your path, your lessons, and you discover what your Soul's name is.

Your Spirit Guides are the higher evolved entities on the Other Side (sometimes known as

Guardian Angels) that guide you and watch over you while you are in this life, on the earth plane. Your Spirit Guides have an unconditional and pure love for you. They also have an intimate knowledge of your path (life's blueprint) from before birth until the day you die – when you rejoin them in our true eternal Home. They are usually present when you are choosing your life's path, experiences and lessons to learn on earth.

Your Spirit Guides will tell you if you are on your correct path, what the future holds and some of the choices you will be facing, as long as it does not interfere with your path. The valuable information they reveal is always for your higher good and for the evolvement of your Soul. Before I see clients for this type of session I recommend bringing a written or typed list of questions because when the client is in this beautiful place of Pure Love, complete happiness and joy, perfect healing, peacefulness and tranquility, they enjoy the positive energy of where they are so much that they forget to ask what they consciously wanted to know.

Just being in the presence of your Spirit Guides helps you to heal and grow. You feel the infinite Pure Love energy of the entire Universe while on the Other Side. You discover so much valuable knowledge and information about yourself, your life, the physical world, and the Other Side. Your mind and Soul are recharged with pure white light love energy. Your mind and Soul are recharged with the awareness of why we are here, what we are supposed to be doing, and where we are going.

∞

One day, a client, Amanda, came to see me to visit the Other Side. She had an overwhelming guilt and was unable to move forward in her life. Happiness seemed to elude her every step of the way since her parents died. She actually had to make the decision to 'pull the plug' on her mother's life support years earlier.

I did a few sessions of hypnosis with her to increase her confidence and enhance her self-image. During the last session with her I guided her to the Other Side. I asked her if she were alone or if others were present. She let me know she was not alone. I directed her to become aware of the most loving, most caring, brightest, most intelligent entity that was near her.   She informed me that one entity came forward.

I asked her if the entity was male or female. She replied, "Male".

"But I don't know who it is.   George, who is it?", Amanda asked, as she was very confused.

"Ask the entity who he is", I encouraged.

"He said his name is John. But I do not know who he is", she reported still being very confused.

I have done this so many times with others, but with her, it seemed a little different. At this point, even though she was in a higher state of awareness, she was being distracted that there was another entity present and not her parents. She really had come to see, and communicate with, her parents. Understanding this, I calmly continued, "I know you came to see your parents.   Sometimes there is a

84

process, and it can be different every time, before a person can visit with their loved ones. What are your feelings, or impressions from John"?

"I feel a lot of love coming from him. I feel so safe and so peaceful", she stated with a confirming and happy voice.

"Ask John who is in relation to you".

"He says he is my Spirit Guide".

We thanked John for speaking with us. We continued with the normal Q&A's about her life and her path. Although she was in a beautiful blissful area she was really interested in seeing her parents.

"Ask John if your parents are available to come and speak with us". The instant I started the question Amanda replied her mother showed up, as John replied, 'yes'.

"George, she is so beautiful. She is really here!" Amanda had tears rolling down her cheeks as her face displayed the happiest smile. "She looks so young and healthy. She is caressing my face telling me she loves me. My mother said it was her time to leave earth when she did."

"Ask your mother if your father is available to come and visit as well".

"She is saying my father is in school right now. He is learning music. She is telling me that they have seen my children". They had passed before Amanda had given birth to her children. "She is saying that my father talks and plays with my son. My mother is saying that they can see us and that they visit our home often."

I gave her time, with my silence, to enjoy her visit with her mother. I also gave her time to gain information, knowledge, and healing while on the Other Side. After this session she was completely transformed. All of the overwhelming guilt was gone and she had an amazing new outlook on life. Her self-confidence and her motivation increased immensely. She would call every now and then over the next few years to thank me and tell me how much that session had done for her.

A few years after that session I was doing a hypnosis show in which I bring the volunteers, at the same time, to the Other Side. She happened to be one of the volunteers. This time both of her parents showed up for the visit. Her father communicated to her that he visits her home often and that he plays with her son. Interestingly, she had called me a year or so after that show. She informed me that when she was at the park with her son he kept laughing. When she was asking him why he was laughing, he would point and say the man keeps doing funny things like a clown. There was no one else there! A few times in the house he would just start laughing, having a lot of fun, as if he were playing with someone. No one else was there! One day she was going through old photos and her son grabbed a picture of her father and said, "Mommy, this is the man who makes me laugh." She had completely forgotten about her visit with her father at my show a year earlier. I reminded her that he told her that he visits often and that he plays with her son. We have it all on video.

∞

In bringing many clients to the Other Side I have discovered, regardless of their belief system, or lack of, they all have similar descriptions of the Other Side. Usually there are at least a few entities, sometimes dozens, sometimes hundreds, who appear to greet the client. Then the Spirit Guides, Guardian Angels, usually always appear to give guidance once I ask the client to become aware of the most loving, most caring, brightest, most intelligent entity near you.

Most of the time the Spirit Guides have been with each client through several lifetimes; sometimes, however, the Spirit Guide is new. For some clients the Spirit Guides come and go depending on numerous and varying factors. Occasionally Spirit Guides choose, or are chosen, to be born on Earth in this physical reality. Sometimes they are promoted to a higher status, or level, to do other work, to teach or train other Guides. They move to other dimensions or worlds to continue to guide in other capacities. Sometimes the client experiences a shift in this life, an advancement or elevation in frequencies/vibrations or perhaps a lower shift that may need a more specialized Spirit Guide because the person is going in directions, a change in path, which is way beyond what could have been expected in a variation.

Most of us have several Spirit Guides at once. There is a hierarchy of Guides; there are the main Guides, then there are supervising guides who oversee the main Guides who are responsible for individuals on Earth who are part of a Soul Circle. A Soul Circle is comprised of the Soul's family, and/or the Soul's close friends, who have been traveling through physical lives on Earth together. And there are Guides, even higher, who oversee the supervising Guides of several Soul circles.

The highest, most evolved, entities on the Other Side sit on the Council of Elders. These entities are of the highest frequencies radiating with the Pure Love Energy of Creation. They do not judge, they are completely free of ego, and have an unconditional and Pure Love for you and the entire Universe. These members are easily in several locations at once. When you are choosing your path for your next life you must go before the Council with your proposed blueprint. With all of their knowledge and wisdom they examine your plans and inform you if your plan may be too difficult, and ultimately if you will be able to handle it. Many times a Soul will go before the Council dozens of times before it is approved. Although they are there to help you and guide you to choose an acceptable path it is still ultimately up to you. If you are determined to enter the next life filled with severe difficulties and lessons, regardless of the Council's suggestions, you can. It is always ultimately up to you.

There are occasions when I guide a client to the Other Side to visit with a loved one and the particular loved one is not available. Sometimes a different loved one will appear, occasionally one that the client never met, even an ancestor. If the loved one is not available usually one of the Spirit Guides appear to inform the client of what the loved one is doing and where that loved one is.

What does that mean when a loved one is not available? They could be learning, working, guiding or perhaps already reborn. On the Other Side everything needed or wanted is, or can be, instantly created. There is no need for money or for food. We are energy. And the energy from Source, all around us and in us, sustains us. Some of what we learn on the Other Side is music, singing, creating, channeling, observing, time shifting/adjusting, various forms of time travel, infinite levels of healing, frequency adjusting, inter dimensional travel, communicating, history and time lines of the infinite realities, recording, and much more!

Only on very rare occasions have entities, loved ones of clients, not crossed over when they come for this type of session. If it is a recent passing I will advise the client to wait, at minimum, a few months. The reason for this is the adjusting phase. Many entities when they first depart this world go through a period of time in which they are helped, by members of their Soul circle and Spirit Guides, to adjust before completely entering the Other Side. The frequencies, the awareness, and the energetic adjustments, for some, can be instantaneous or take several months of Earth time.

Each Soul is different and the adjusting period depends on an almost infinite number of factors. One of the main factors is the Soul's level of evolvement. Another factor affecting the waiting period is how they passed. Sometimes a traumatic passing, especially if the person was not meant to pass in that fashion or at that time, can take longer to adjust.

One time, a woman had called to make an appointment to visit her husband on the Other Side. Unfortunately, he had passed within the last six weeks. I explained to her that he might not be available, but she just did not want to wait. Her husband was her world and he had been taken from her suddenly and unexpectedly. When I guided her to the Other Side her Spirit Guide appeared and explained to her that, not only was he not available, but he actually had not crossed over yet. Her Spirit Guide informed her that her husband was concerned about their daughter and was watching over her. The husband did not realize he would be more effective in watching over his daughter from the Other Side. However, he had died before his time and did not want to cross over until he was certain that his daughter was going to be ok.

Even when a Soul has not crossed over yet, it is still possible to communicate. Depending on the client's level of evolvement, and the ability to go to the higher states of awareness that communication is very possible. Unfortunately for this particular client she was not at a level that would afford her that opportunity. Her Spirit Guide explained that she would be unable to communicate with him, also, because the husband was not at a specific level and was pretty much closed off to everything except the daughter. Her Spirit Guide did tell her that she would be able to communicate with him, on the Other Side, in the future, when he does eventually cross over.

Receiving all of this information I decided to do a regression. I had already brought the woman into the higher states of awareness, although this session would be different than the usual regressions I do: regressing someone while in the higher states of awareness is another approach, sometimes an even more effective approach. Her Spirit Guide agreed that it would be ok to do the regression and the client was excited to do it.

Remember, when doing a regression in hypnosis you are not just remembering the events, but it is as though you are reliving the event with all of your senses and awareness. I had her bring up the happiest feelings that she had ever felt, as much as she could. In hypnosis all senses are heightened; so when she was feeling the feeling of happiness more than she had ever felt it, I had her hold onto that feeling and follow it back in time to the happiest moment she had experienced with her husband. As I counted back from ten to one allowing her to follow the feeling, her awareness moved back in time. When I reached the number one I commanded her, "Be there now".

She was back in time experiencing, as though for the first time, a moment with her husband. He was holding her in his arms as they were gazing into each other's eyes. For her, this was a blissful moment and she was now re-experiencing it! When she emerged, even though she had not gotten to visit with her husband's departed Soul, she felt at peace and happy. In the session she was in the presence of her Spirit Guide who let her know that her husband is waiting to cross over because he is concerned about their daughter. She now knows that she will be with her husband again when she departs this world, and this life is just a blink of an eye in eternity. She was so grateful that she was able to relive a special moment with her husband. The experience was very healing for her on many levels.

Depending on the level of evolvement of the client/student I will also use a technique of shifting time to the future, while in the higher states of awareness, to allow a visit with a loved one. Recently, a client wanted to visit with her cousin who had passed away several months prior to the session. While she was on the Other Side her Spirit Guide informed her that her cousin was not yet adjusted, was still in a transition period, and was not available for direct communication. So I had her inform her Guide that I intended to shift her awareness to a future period on the Other Side in which her cousin will be adjusted and available to communicate. I also had her ask the Spirit Guide if it would be ok to do so, and if he would assist us with the process. With permission we brought her awareness to a future period on the Other Side to visit with her cousin.

The client loved it! She was able to speak with her cousin as if no time had passed at all. The cousin, on the Other Side, was aware of the shift and the time difference of this visit. He informed her that, although she was in my office on that particular date, her awareness was communicating with him almost a year, in human/earthly terms, in the future. For her, not only was she able to communicate with a loved one who had passed away, but she was now open to even more infinite possibilities. After the session, wiping her tears, she exclaimed, "Anything really is possible!" With a big smile she affirmed what I had said to her before the session.

∞

Just a quick note on spirits who have not crossed over: when doing hypnosis sessions to eliminate/correct certain issues, there are times when I come across 'attachments'. Mainly these attachments are spirits, who for various reasons, have not crossed over, or who have refused to cross over. They attach themselves to people, who are very unaware, using their energy and many times influencing thoughts, actions, and behaviors. Many times it is a departed spirit of a person who had a drug addiction or alcohol addiction who attaches to a living person with a substance abuse problem, usually when the living person is in a very weakened state.

Most attachments are not of a maleficent nature. Sometimes it is a loved one who has recently passed and wishes to 'help' the person to whom they are attached. Once this is discovered I do a de-possession. I will communicate with the attached spirits and then I guide them to the Other Side. Sometimes there are hundreds of attached spirits, but they all can be effectively addressed. When the de-possession is completed, the issues that the living client was experiencing are now gone. The issues range from all sorts of anxieties, depression, bad habits, allergies, phobias, and addictions. Dr. Edith Fiore has written an insightful book on the subject of attachments called, "The Unquiet Dead", if you would like to explore the topic in more depth.

∞

Shortly after my Grandma Gerry passed away, I was bringing my youngest brother to the movies. We had time before the movie started so I asked him if he would like to do hypnosis. Once I had him in the deepest states of hypnosis, without telling him what I was going to do, I separated his mind from his body and guided him to the higher states of awareness and then through the tunnel onto the Other Side.

"Are you alone or are you with others?" I asked.

He did not answer. His face became red and tears starting rolling down his cheeks. He did not verbally respond, when asked, but instead he nodded his head confirming that he was not alone. Not wanting to interfere with his experience by pressing him into a response of who was with him, I gave him time in silence saying, "Enjoy your time, share your love, receive any information that will help you in this life, in the moment of silence which begins now..."

When I emerged him from hypnosis, as he was wiping his tears, he described his experience. He informed me that our grandmother, Gerry, was there, glowing, looking much younger and much healthier than when she had passed away. She was smiling and telling him that she is ok. She is very happy in a beautiful place. She was watching over him and for him not to worry about her and not to be sad. Dying is not the end. We exist eternally, she told him, so be happy. Then she said she had to go and hugged him.

One night I was guiding myself, through self-hypnosis, to the higher states of awareness, to connect to Source to do healing. I went through the tunnel and into the light of the Other Side. As soon as I emerged from the tunnel onto the Other Side I was directly in front of my Grandmother Gerry. On her right side was Jesus, and on her left was Mary, and behind them, a sea of glowing people. There was no end to the amount of people standing behind them.

My entire being was vibrating with high frequencies, powerful feelings of love and gratitude. The sea of people was saying "thank you" - thanking me for being who I am and what I was doing on Earth. With all of my energy I sent love and gratitude back to them and the entire Universe. It was an amazing experience! When I emerged I was filled with joy and felt so much peace in every part of my being. I did not get to my healing work that evening, but I assumed, at the time, that they were thanking me for the healing work that I do.

∞

Besides going to the Other Side countless times throughout my life, almost every day as an adult, and guiding countless clients to the Other Side to have extraordinary experiences there are still just too many skeptics. This information comes from countless individuals in private and group sessions. These people are from various backgrounds and dramatically different belief systems, people of all ages and all walks of life, people who are skeptic and who adamantly reject an afterlife. They all see, feel, hear, and experience, with all of their senses, this beautiful place of pure love, complete happiness and joy. They all communicate with loved ones and/or Spirit Guides. The biggest skeptics are not only dramatically transformed into believers, but are transformed into individuals who know with absolute certainty of the Other Side and our true infinite and eternal nature.

Of course, there are individuals who are adamantly against even wanting to know or experience the possibilities of there being more to this physical world. Skeptics can be cautiously open to other possibilities of things outside of their valued belief system. The skeptics I am referring to right now are not the ones who just disbelieve, but the ones who absolutely refuse to be open to the possibility. Their belief system tells them that this is a physical world and there is nothing else. They believe strongly that when you die, you're dead and that's that. You just no longer exist. They are the ones who say the Other Side exists only in the minds of people who want to believe in something that just is not real.

I would never attempt to persuade these people whatsoever. When these individuals vehemently exclaim to me that it is just a person's imagination, and none of what they experience is 'real', I would just say that if it is real or not it does not matter. The benefits for, the transformations of, every client who experience these sessions are just so great - it does not matter if it is just their imagination.

Why argue? I know how real it is; however, regardless of how much proof and evidence you present to the super skeptic they refuse to accept anything that goes against their chosen belief systems. Many times, the super-skeptic presents, in their argument, outdated, and mis-learned theories of information that is utilized to keep them subjected to the ridiculous limitations that society requires of its subjects. They will exclaim scientific proof without any investigation or substantial evidence. When they try to use science as the explanation they only utilize what a 'normal' person is told what they are supposed to believe. They absolutely refuse to consider, or acknowledge all of the actual scientific evidence that now confirms the reality of much of what they are arguing against.

One of my aunts is a prime example of the super skeptic. She believes it may be possible for hypnosis to work if the issue is not of a physical nature and is only an issue of the mind. In doing hypnosis as long as I have, and having access to higher knowledge and understanding, I know with absolute certainty that everything of a physical nature is associated with, influenced by, if not controlled by, the mind. Your mind is so very powerful. I love to guide my clients to get out of their own way to realize the true infinite power of their mind. What the mind imagines the body feels. What the mind imagines the body realizes. I presented, to my aunt, actual people and documented testimonials of amazing physical healing through hypnosis sessions. She only had theories of what she had been taught. My aunt was almost on the verge of violence because her belief system, her idea of reality, was seriously being challenged. Her main contention was that if what I was saying were true, they would shut down all of the hospitals and there would no longer be any need for doctors. Yes. Unfortunately it all depends on a person's belief system.

There have been countless studies of the placebo effect. People have successfully cured "incurable" diseases with placebo pills. It is not the pill, but it is the power of the mind that does the actual healing of the physical body. When you believe a pill is going to work, your body begins to adjust in readiness to be healed. When you expect, once you take the pill, that it is going to heal you, you begin to heal. What the mind imagines, the body feels. When you believe and expect that the pill will heal you, your body adjusts to what your mind imagines, your body allows the healing to be realized. When you KNOW the pill is healing you - you are healed that much quicker. When you know that you are healing, the healing is a reality and your physical body responds.

If you believe you can or you believe you cannot, you are absolutely right. If you believe you will be healed or you believe you cannot be healed - you are absolutely right. Also, there are no side effects to the placebo. Interestingly, they have done placebo effect studies listing all of the 'possible' side effects. Some of those side effects listed were: nausea, headaches, vomiting, fainting, dizziness, and more. The subjects being 'aware' of the possible, negative, side effects started displaying the adverse effects. Once they had taken the pill some began to have headaches. Others were dizzy, nauseous and experienced other side effects. They had taken a sugar pill for which there are no adverse side effects. Why did that happen? The subjects believed, imagined or thought, that they would experience those side effects, and they did. What the mind imagines the body feels. Whatever your mind thinks about or imagines will manifest in various ways in your physical body.

Much of what Jesus said when he was on Earth teaching and healing many has been deleted and misinterpreted. The only thing that I will point out here is what Jesus taught about belief and healing. Many, especially Christians, think that Jesus said you have to believe in him to be healed. He did not. Jesus said all you have to do to be healed is to believe. Believe you will be healed and you will be healed. Your mind is so very powerful, but sometimes you may need something or someone to have you focus your mind, imagination, thoughts, to be directed to your healing; for example, crystals, hypnotist, energy healer, doctor, acupuncturist, or a healer of any modality, or any item or object to direct your focus and belief. Everything works - if you believe it will, if you expect it to, if you know it.

Going back to the story of my aunt; I was trying very hard not to have this conversation with her, but she persisted. I tried to explain that it is ok for her to believe as she does, and that I am not trying to convince her of anything. We all have our beliefs and our own idea of reality and that I was ok with that. However, that was not good enough for her. She wanted to convince me to believe what she believes only because that is what she believes. She wanted me to accept her reality. Can we not just agree that we do not agree and be ok with that and respect that? Not acceptable for her.

My aunt then wanted to discuss the Other Side regardless of me saying that I am not trying to convince her of anything. I let her know that I am more than ok with her not believing in what I do, but that what I do is absolutely real. Again, I have countless real clients and students who have been to the Other Side and back through private sessions and workshops with me. I have countless written and video testimonials. And not only have I guided clients, students, friends, and family members to the Other Side, I have personally been there, and continue to go there all of the time. Her father, my grandfather on my birth father's side, had recently passed. She demanded if the Other Side were real why I have not visited her father. My reply was, "I go there all of the time. My Grandmother Gerry who was the only person, when alive, from whom I received any real love from, is not always available. I had visited with her a few times and brought other family members to visit with her on the Other Side. I am on auto pilot. I go where I am needed to do healing work. If an entity on the Other Side, family members included, need me, or need to inform me of something, they will". I continued to try to explain to my aunt, "I personally have no reason to visit with him, but if he needs to see me he will. Also, he may not be available; it is possible for him to have already been reborn". Although her face was turning a deeper shade of red with other signs of her visible anger, I continued, "If you would like to visit him I am more than happy to guide you to the Other Side to see him or at least discover where he is right now."

This absolutely infuriated her. For her, this was proof that it was not real. She refused to agree to experience it. She refused to accept the countless testimonials of clients' and students' experiences. It did not make sense to her why I had no interest in visiting her father. However, I never had any type of relationship with her father, my grandfather. Growing up I had lived on the same street as my aunt. My grandfather would walk right by me, turning his head, in front of my house, on his way to my aunt's house, and he did not even say hello. He completely ignored me. As an adult, I thought that maybe he behaved in that manner because of my mother who could be less than welcoming. That was not the reason though; he just had no interest, for whatever reason, in me or my brother, the biological children of his son. And that is ok.

The episode with my Aunt was several years ago and I have not been invited back to her home since. I do continue to send her Love, Light, and Happiness with my pure positive intentions.

∞

Everything works; if you believe it, if you expect it, and most importantly if you KNOW it! A regular session of hypnosis can work miracles for you. With the metaphysical hypnosis sessions you are opened up to the infinite possibilities and extraordinary reality of who you really are. Whether you visit the Other Side, explore the many facets of astral travel, fly to perfection through dream control, visit previous lives, or lives between lives you can have any and all of the perfection you desire. Once you are exposed to the ease in which you can tap into the infinite intelligence and eternal wisdom of the entire universe you begin to transcend the heaviness of this physical world.

I know how absolutely real all of this is. I know how powerful your mind is! I know you are an amazing, powerful, and perfect being of light! I know you are an infinite and eternal being of Pure Love. My goal is for you to KNOW how amazing and how perfect you are because once you are absolutely aware of who you are - you will no longer suffer with anything, you will heal and adjust to your perfection, you will accept that life can be easy and enjoyable, and you will co-create a beautiful world going forward!

Maybe I am getting ahead of myself. I am just really excited for you, even if you are already aware of your infinite self, to experience the beauty, the joy, the perfection, the Pure Love, and the absolute reality of your eternal home on the Other Side.

CHAPTER 7: ABSOLUTE PROOF

"Learning the lessons of life can be so simple if you believe in immortality."

- Brian L. Weis

"Believe it! Expect it! KNOW it!"

- Geozuwa

A 16 year old girl named Page had come to see me, with the permission of her foster parents, for a hypnosis session. She wanted to have more confidence, and to be happier. Her foster parents wanted her to be less rebellious and to eliminate her self-destructive behaviors. The girl needed to make better choices.

Page was pleasant and respectful; however, you could see, or sense, a roughness, an edge with deep pain behind her smile. In the information gathering portion of our meeting I discovered, confirmed by the foster parents, that her mother was a drug addicted prostitute. Page's mother used her to gain favor and barter for drugs by allowing the drug dealers to use Page for sex beginning at the age of twelve. She had experienced some of the toughest physical and emotional abuse.

Feeling this girl's pain, I had to continue to fight back tears before placing her into a deep state of hypnosis. As I was deepening her into hypnosis I was giving her suggestions of healing and positive reinforcements.   I had her bring up the feeling associated with why she was in my office.   As she brought up the feeling as much as she could, I regressed her to the last time she experienced that feeling.   She had met her mother's new drug dealer, knowing what was expected of her.   Her mother had set this up from the distance so she could bargain and attain her drugs hopefully, for free.   She depended on her daughter to follow through for her.   The girl had feelings of fear, anger, hatred, guilt, shame, and betrayal.   She also felt obligated to help her mother, because her mother "needed her".   Page's sub-conscious mind felt she had an obligation to always prove her value to her mother, although it was a distorted sense of worth that was instilled in her by her mother from the earliest ages.

I then regressed her to the first time she experienced the feelings.   She was a baby in the crib. She could hear the fighting of her parents in the next room.   The baby was terrified and thought she was going to die.   The father was yelling about killing the baby, and the mother was telling the father it would be ok.   The mother was saying that she did not want the baby, the girl they already had (her older sister) was the most important.   This baby, Page, was the product of the mother getting pregnant from one of their drug dealers.

After the regression the girl realized why she was experiencing the things she was experiencing. She became aware that she felt and acted the way she did as a result of certain events in her past. Although, before the session, she had thought that she was in control of the choices she made. She thought that she was being tough and that she could handle anything. She now realized that much of what she did for her mother was to always prove her worth, subconsciously knowing that her parents did not want her.   We then did all of the forgiveness work necessary to heal.   She forgave her mother, her father, the drug dealers and she forgave herself. Forgiveness is our most powerful healing tool.

Because of the amazing success and tremendous benefits, with all of the clients I bring to the Other Side and back, I decided to guide her to the Other Side.   With the use of hypnosis I guided her through the bright glowing tunnel into the brilliant white light on the other end of the tunnel.   She was now in an area of Pure Love, absolute forgiveness, complete happiness and joy - a beautiful area of pure positive energy, an area of healing.   The healing that occurs in this area is, many times, instantaneous, and fully effective on all levels - spiritual, energetic, emotional, physical, and more.

She was enjoying the peacefulness, the joy, and the energy that surrounded her.   The physical signs of what she was experiencing were evident.   As I had done with many clients before, I guided her to become aware of the most loving, most caring, brightest, most intelligent entities near her.   Although, it was difficult for her to speak, she confirmed that there were many loving entities all around her.   Giving her the guidance to take control of her vocal chords she then became clearer in communicating with me.   I had her become aware of the most loving, most caring, brightest, most intelligent entity near her. One entity came forward as the others made way.

"Are you familiar with this entity?" I asked as I normally do.

"Yes", she replied.

I continued with the next usual question, "What relation does the entity have with you?"

She quickly replied, "She is my Spirit Guide".

At this point I must mention that although the girl is very intelligent and knows how to read, she had never read a book. She had never been to church, and did not know anything about religion. Up to this point she had never consciously heard of a Spirit Guide. She did not know anything about Heaven, or the Other Side. All she knew, or cared about, on the surface anyway, was which boy she was going to choose to be with which weekend, or how she was going to get alcohol. She was completely unaware of who I was and she had absolutely no knowledge of my history or any of my experiences. The only thing she knew about me was that I am a hypnotist.

"What is your Spirit Guide's name?" I continued.

"Sheena".

"How long has she been your Spirit Guide", I asked, because for some individuals, their Spirit Guides come and go, with others they have remained for thousands of lifetimes. Page responded, for her Guide, "Many lifetimes", as she also relayed to me that her Guide was familiar with me and had actually been a friend of mine on the Other Side for a very long time.

While working with my clients in hypnosis, I have done this before several times. Bringing clients to the higher states of awareness to gain valuable information about their lives and paths is my favorite type of session to do. Having clients face to face with loved ones who have passed or their Spirit Guides is always so amazing for the client and for me. Now with Page, I was about to do something that I had never done before.

"Page, ask Sheena if she wouldn't mind coming in for a while to speak with me directly". I quickly received an affirmative response and proceeded. "Tell Sheena I am going to count from one to three and tap you on your forehead. On the count of three and the tap on your forehead I want you to completely allow Sheena to come in and speak with me. Tell Sheena to let me know when she is in".

Slowly and softly I counted, "one...two...three". I began to rapidly tap her forehead as I reached the number three exclaiming, "Now let her completely in to speak with me".

Her eyes, under her eyelids began to flutter while her body was shaking. Then her body, and her face, suddenly went still, and a distinguishably different voice said a soft and peaceful, "*Hello*".

"Hello, who am I speaking with"? I asked with utter curiosity and amazement.

"*Sheena*"

"And who are you"? I continued to ask with fascination.

"*I am her Spirit Guide*"

"Where is the girl?"

"She is no longer in her body, she is higher."

Further, Sheena proceeded to tell me that she guided Page to come see me because she was seriously considering suicide. I was quickly more concerned and asked her how I can help her. She informed me that the hypnosis session I had already done with her has helped and that she would not be committing suicide.

Since this was my first experience of having a client completely channel a higher evolved entity, a Spirit Guide, I began a series of questions. I wanted answers to all the great questions with no middleman. I wanted the answers without any physical beings' interpretations or maps of reality. Because of my Catholic upbringing I also asked if suicide is against the rules. Sheena said that it is. She said if a person commits suicide they must be reborn.

The information I was receiving from Sheena during our conversation was fascinating. When we pass from this life we are not judged by anyone. We are not judged by God! We judge ourselves! And who is our worst critic? Yes, we are, usually, our worst critic.

Sheena explained to me that Page chose the exact path that she was on. If she had committed suicide she would have been reborn to experience the same type of life again. She told me she was present with the girl as she was deciding on a path. Initially she was choosing a much more difficult and painful path to experience.

Most of us choose the paths, the life, the parents, and mostly everything we experience in this physical life. When we are in our true Home, on the Other Side, in our true perfection, our Souls feel invincible. So when we choose to experience life we sometimes choose the most difficult and painful paths. After all, one hundred years of life on Earth is shorter than a blink of an eye on the Other Side. Luckily we have to bring our plans for life before the Council of Elders. These wise evolved Masters will reject initial plans, sometimes dozens of times, before they agree that the particular Soul will be able to handle the life and path they are choosing.

Continuing to impart information to me, Sheena confirmed that the girl chose her mother, chose the abuse, the pain, and all of the difficulties she was experiencing. She also told me that the Girl was of a higher power. The girl was able to completely channel because she had practiced in her previous life and on the Other Side. Her Soul was evolved high enough, combined with the training, to be able to channel.

Sheena informed me that she was familiar with me, and that she knows me from before this life. She started naming my Spirit Guides after I asked her if she knew them. Then I asked her if one of them was available to come in and speak to me now. After the affirmative response, letting me know that my Spirit Guide Sofi was available, I told her I was going to count from one - three and tap on the forehead. "On the count of three and the tap on the forehead allow Sofi to come in and have her let me know when she is in".

I began to count, from one to three. When I reached the number three I began to tap the forehead and the body began shaking, and the eyes were fluttering, just like before.

"*Hello*", came a soft angelic voice different sounding from the voice of Sheena when she was inside Page's body. Sofi, my Spirit Guide was now inside this girl speaking to me directly with no interference! I began to ask questions, also keeping my "scientific/logical" mind present, not just accepting this as completely real. However, Sofi started telling me things about myself, my experiences, that no other person on this planet knows except me. Not a friend, no family member, no relationship whatsoever could possibly have known these things except me. She told me she had been with me when certain events had happened, and described those events on several occasions at various ages. Trying to trip her up, I said, "So when such and such happened to me when I was nine years old, you were there?" Sofi quickly responded that such and such happened when I was actually eleven years old and yes, she had been there. After all of my experiences, throughout my life, this was the absolute turning point. This was now, for me, absolute certainty! I continued with numerous questions.

I asked if people born on Earth choose their paths and their experiences before they are born. Sofi explained that most entities on the Other Side continue to learn and grow and sometimes experience a physical life on Earth that allows a Soul to learn and grow quicker than remaining on the Other

Side for a longer period of time. A Soul will begin to map out a blueprint for an up-coming life, in which they want to experience a learning and growing process to evolve their Soul. The entity can choose on their own, but usually incorporate the assistance of their particular Soul Circle and their Spirit Guides. A Soul Circle is a group of entities, Soul Family and Soul Friends that are related in that they continue to travel together through physical lives, and continue to watch over one another when not in the physical life together.

Once the Soul has created a certain life path to follow they will present this blueprint in front of the Council of Elders. The Council of Elders are a group of Ultra-Evolved Master Souls in tune with Infinite Intelligence and possessing vast wisdom. The Council will review the plan and make suggestions for alterations before being approved to be born or reborn. A Soul will, usually, design a very tough and painful path to experience. The Other Side is a beautiful perfect place of Pure Love with no judgement and no ego. When you are residing on the Other Side between lives, you feel invincible and believe you can handle anything a physical life can throw at you. Also, a hundred years of a physical life on Earth is equivalent to a blink of an eye on the Other Side. Sometimes a Soul will go in front of the Council dozens of times before a suitable life path is approved.

If you take a moment to review your life and your experiences, you may want to give the Council a deserved acknowledgement of gratitude. Life can be very tough. And most likely you chose the difficult experiences or events in your life. Imagine if the Council approved the first life path you chose. How difficult would that path have been? The Council approves your path according to what they, in their infinite wisdom, believe you can handle. Ultimately, however, it is up to you. You do not have to accept their suggestions and you may choose the exact life, with all of the pain and suffering that you want.

Sofi explained to me I am on my correct path and doing everything I am supposed to be doing. Perhaps I will reveal more about my path with you as you read further into this book. But briefly I am here on Earth to evolve the Souls of as many as possible, to heal many, to teach, to write enlightening books, to bring awareness of the Other Side, and to wake you up to your true infinite and eternal self. I am also here to empower children to know who they are from the earliest ages by creating, building, and establishing a Healing and Learning Center for Children. I am here to end the cycles of dysfunction and eliminate hatred and abuse. It sounds like a lot, but I am confident that I will accomplish all of my goals and I know that many of you will assist me.

With the information of choosing paths, and how Page chose the horrible things she experienced, for confirmation, I asked Sofi, "Sheena told me Page chose all of the abuse, her experiences, and her situations. So I chose to experience the abuse and torture I experienced from my stepfather as well?" With a very stern, much louder, tone of voice, Sofi replied "*NO! NO! NO!*" Of course this threw me off.

The abuse I experienced was a huge part of my life; it colored and shaped a lot of who I am. I always felt that I was the strong confident person I am because of those experiences. As the common saying goes, "What does not kill you makes you stronger". I always assumed, like most people who believe in reincarnation, that we choose our paths. Very concerned, and a little disoriented, I asked Sofi, "If I didn't choose the abuse, what happened? Why did I experience it?"

Sofi, very solemnly, replied, "*You were pushed out of the way*".

"What does that mean?" I wanted to know!

Sofi seemed concerned, "*An evil entity pushed you out of the way to take your place in the family you were supposed to have been born to*".

At this point I was not feeling that great. How could this be allowed to happen? Why did my Guides not step in? My mind was racing, and I wanted answers! However, Sofi could not stay in Page's body any longer. This session had already been over three hours in duration. Sofi said, "*I must go now.*"

"Will you be available in the future to come in and speak with me again"? I asked quickly.

"*Yes*".

"Thank you again for coming in and speaking with me. I greatly appreciate it. With all of my gratitude go with love and allow the girl to come back in her body".

When Page reentered her body, her mind was still in those higher states of awareness. She was still on the Other Side, when I began to speak to her again: "Take another look around, and know with absolute certainty you can come to these areas and even higher, every time we do this. And every time we do this you are much more aware, each and every time, much more aware than the time before. In a moment I am going to count down from ten to one. With every count, you leave from where you are now and by the time I reach the number six or five you merge with your physical body remembering everything you have experienced, everything you have learned, sharing with your physical brain, the healing, the knowledge, and the wisdom."

"And one, so deeply relaxed feeling wonderful in every way. Mind and body relaxing, together, perfectly, so deeply........"

Upon emerging her from hypnosis I asked her many questions about her experiences. She said she was in this beautiful, peaceful place, which seemed like a park, with hundreds and hundreds of people staring at her. She did not feel any fear. She said she felt a lot of love coming from them, and she felt very safe and protected. Everyone was dressed in white; there were old people, young people, hundreds of people with bright glowing energy all around them. She then described Sheena as this beautiful woman, appearing to be around thirty years old, with flowing hair and the warmest, most loving, smile. The girl also let me know that she was not present at all during the entire time I was speaking to the Spirit Guides. Page had no awareness of any part of my conversations. She also did not have an awareness of Sofi. I was speaking to the Guides inside of her for over three hours. She said she felt like she was on the Other Side with all of those beings for only five minutes. I had not given her any suggestions of time distortion, but time had been shifted.

She very happily informed me how wonderful she felt. She described having this new lighter feeling, and everything seemed to be brighter. I asked her if she would come back to do it again. As she leaned over, her eyes a little teary, she whispered, "Yes, definitely".

I was excited for the girl to come back and to speak with my Spirit Guide again. I was writing down all of my questions. One thing was concerning me and weighing on my mind: I had never heard of an entity pushing another's Soul out of the way to take their place. I made inquiries to others who were supposed to be enlightened, individuals claiming to be spiritual teachers, but there were no satisfactory responses. They were all way too unfamiliar with what I was doing. They were confused and tried to brush things off, not knowing how to respond. For instance, one person told me that it was impossible. I was told that entities cannot "push" an incoming Soul "out of the way" from being born, and that the entity or girl had lied to me. Another example of what I was told, was that if an entity were saying that to you, it must not be working from the light. These two examples were from people that just did not understand or they were just entrenched in their limited belief systems or trainings. The answers I appreciated the most were from individuals who admitted that they were completely unfamiliar with these types of experiences.

I knew how real my experience had been, and how it was absolutely impossible for anything less than pure, positive, and loving to enter in order to communicate with me. I knew with absolute certainty it was my Spirit Guide temporarily inside Page's body, giving me true information. The information and accounts of my life she had related to me were only known by me. There was no reason for me to think, not even for a second, that I was being, or could be, mislead. In any case, I was eager for Page to return so I could discover exactly what had taken place and why.

Page came back several times. Each time we did this it would last around three hours and it would only feel like five minutes for her. After I explain to you what she had said concerning me being pushed out of the way before my birth I will condense our conversations into some of the valuable information.

During the next visit, once Page was in a deep state of hypnosis and guided to the Other Side I counted and tapped her forehead, the body was shaking, the eyes fluttered, similar to the previous times, I heard, "*Hello.*"

I confirmed that it was Sofi back inside of the body of Page. After thanking her for coming in to speak with me I immediately, and eagerly, began to ask all of my questions. I needed answers about being moved right before birth.

Sofi informed me that an evil entity moved me out of the way so that the entity could exact revenge on the family to which I was supposed to be born. It was a wealthy family. Sofi explained to me that she knew the family, but I was not allowed to know who they are.

I had to be born when I was born. So I was born to a different family. To add a little more interest to this story, from the moment I could speak I would tell my mother, and family members, that she was not my mother. I used to say I was from another world, and that I had been zapped into her stomach. I was one or two years old and that was the language I used. And my family continues, to this day, to joke around and say that I always thought I was an alien.

The incidents around my birth are even more interesting because of what I discovered after that session during a barbecue at my mother's house. I found out for the first time, I was never told this before, or if I was, I did not remember being told. At my mother's barbecue she was telling stories of her past. One of her stories was about her pregnancy with me. My mother weighed 98 pounds, continued to have a normal menstrual cycle, no morning sickness, with no symptoms of being pregnant whatsoever. She had a serious cold or flu so my grandparents took her to the doctor. The Doctor informed her that she was six months pregnant. This fact was confirmed by my grandmother and my uncles. A few weeks after receiving the news she gave birth to me.

Sofi explained that was why Jesus came to visit me when he did. He came to visit me to let me know I was about to experience things in this life that I was not meant to experience. At hearing this I was even more excited. If you remember my first beautiful Jesus experience in Chapter two, I never had a conscious awareness of why Jesus came to visit me or of what had been said.

Before proceeding I must clarify one thing. In bringing clients to the Other Side many times before my interaction with Sofi, some clients would relay that the entity in front of them had been Jesus. Sometimes the Pure Love coming from the entity before them is so powerful and so beautiful their senses interpret it as coming from Jesus. I will request that client to ask, "What is the entity's name?", and usually the image changes and the entity is, many times, a Spirit Guide, or a highly evolved loved one. On rare occasions it is in fact Jesus! To confirm that it is Jesus, I ask for a personal message to be relayed to me that only I and Jesus know.

So when Sofi was telling me she was there when Jesus came to visit me I asked if it was actually Jesus. She confirmed that my Jesus experience was authentic. Sofi informed me that Jesus came to see me because I was about to experience things in this lifetime that I was not meant to experience. All I had to do was just get through it. I had important work to do in this life. It made sense to me, because shortly after Jesus visited me my stepfather came into the picture. He unleashed such hatred, abuse, and torture on me. During the time in the same house with my stepfather I would pray for death, for God to just take me away. I cried myself to sleep many nights. On my knees, crying, I begged my mother to please stop him from hitting me.

Sofi said I was not supposed to experience any abuse at all. It was not part of my path. Interestingly, she said she had not helped me in choosing my path. She further explained that I had not actually chosen my path, but instead, I was chosen. Apparently I am a member of the Council of Xeruwan Beings, a member of the Inter-Galactic, Inter Dimensional Council, the first children of God created, and that the Council of Elders for human beings on the Other Side, chose me to come to Earth to teach, to heal, and to evolve the Souls of as many people as possible. Part of my mission in this life is to bring absolute awareness of the Other Side to everyone. I am here to wake people up to their true infinite and eternal self. By the way, there are more chosen ones, Christed ones, being born now than at any other time in human existence. Now is a crucial point in the current perceived time line of Earth for the evolution and ascension of humans.

Sometimes when a higher evolved entity, such as a Spirit Guide, communicates with humans in this physical reality it can be quite overwhelming to all of the human senses. First, the Guides have to slow down their frequencies and vibrations enough to adjust to the appropriate time, space, and form of communication. Quite often they are very literal and very formal when they speak. Clarification of words and meanings are, many times, necessary. Sometimes the Spirit Guides, depending on their level of evolvement, or their training skill level, find it difficult to explain certain answers in human terms;

terms that can be understood with our language and human interpretations.

Often, questions from a human perspective have no meaning, or a meaning that just makes no sense to an evolved understanding. Questions that may seem paramount to humans actually make no sense to even ask. So the higher evolved Spirit Guides must study to interpret what is really being asked or how to respond to give proper information when needed. For example, think about asking someone, "What is the marital status of the number seven?" The number seven is not married. So the number seven is a bachelor? Well, no it is not a bachelor. Is the number seven divorced or widowed? The number seven is not married, but it does not fit into those other categories either. It does not make sense to even ask the question. Although some of the questions asked do not make sense, the Spirit Guides, with no judgement and infinite patience, will answer every question with love in the best possible manner to help and guide you while on Earth.

Having Sofi, my Spirit Guide, communicating directly with me, through Page was a real life changing experience for me. These sessions, for me, were a defining moment in my life and my vision. I now had absolute confirmation of my purpose in this life. When you truly discover and are aware of your specific purpose it is so freeing, amazing, and empowering.

After Sofi, my Spirit Guide, channeled through Page, revealed to me who I am and my purpose in this life, I received an abundance of confirmations from everywhere. Being told by another Guide, channeled through another person, the same information that Sofi had presented to me would have been enough of a confirmation. However, several clients and students relayed information to me from their Spirit Guides, or their Spirit Guides channeled through with information, that confirmed what Sofi had revealed to me, without being asked. Homeless people in New York City would suddenly stop doing whatever they were doing, turn to me, and specifically state information about me that Sofi had shared with me. Individuals who had no prior knowledge of me with heightened psychic abilities would just begin telling me certain information about me confirming Sofi's information.

Sofi said that my grandmother Gerry was not available when I asked to speak with her. My grandmother was not reborn, but she was guiding on Earth. She was not officially a Spirit Guide, but a level right below. Grandma Gerry was a Spirit Guide in training. At that moment, and for some time, she was on Earth, in spirit form, guiding a girl named Maria in New Jersey. Sofi informed me that when I went to the Other Side and saw her with Jesus and the sea of people, that was immediately prior to Grandma Gerry going into training and that she would not be available for a while. However, she would be able to speak with me in this format eventually. It took a couple of years, but I have since visited with her on the Other Side.

∞

Before my visits with Grandma Gerry and before Sofi came through to speak to me in this manner, but after my grandmother had passed - my aunt Lisa, Grandma Gerry's daughter-in-law, began to have strange occurrences everyday around twelve noon. Her TV would turn on by itself on the classic movie channel with black and white movies playing. At first these occurrences were spooking her. She and witnesses began to note the specific channel on the TV when it was turned off for the night. Of course, no one in her house, including her, watched the classic movie channels. But sure enough, the following day around noon the TV would turn on by itself tuned to the classic movie channel with a black and white movie playing.

Lisa described the events to her niece, who was visiting for the day. As she was sharing the TV experiences of the past couple of weeks to her niece, around 11:45 a.m. - the TV turned on, by itself and it was unplugged! The TV was tuned to the classic channel and a black and white movie playing. Her niece screamed.

My family contacted me. It seemed as though it was Grandma Gerry attempting to communicate. My grandmother loved the old black and white movies and enjoyed watching the classic movie channels before she had passed away. She, perhaps, had an urgent message. I guided Lisa to the Other Side. Her facial expressions changed, her face was red, and she had tears. She was telling me that she was alone. I was confused and asked her if she were enjoying where she was - she was. Being on the

Other Side is very healing on so many levels. I decided to allow her to stay there for a while and enjoy where she was. I figured she could not go any higher or maybe my grandmother was no longer available to communicate.

Lisa, later after the hypnosis session, in confidence, explained to me, that her ex-husband had appeared. Her ex-husband had passed several years earlier from an accident during a high speed police chase. She did not want to tell me while she was on the Other-Side because she did not want to make my uncle jealous. She told me that she really enjoyed the visit and that she had learned a lot from it. She had given forgiveness to her husband for everything he had done when he was alive and for having left her in such an abrupt fashion. Forgiveness is always for you. Sometimes entities will come through knowing that you need to forgive them, for you to move forward and to heal.

Some time later, Sofi confirmed that it was my grandmother Gerry who was turning the TV on at my uncle's house. She said that she had a private message for my uncle. Grandma Gerry had not appeared to Lisa for a number of reasons. First: the message was private for my uncle. Second: Lisa did not want to see my grandmother. Third: it was very important for Lisa and her ex-husband to meet at that time for mutual healing.

Sofi confirmed that she had been there, and it had been real, when my great grandmother May had visited me and Grandma Gerry when I was a child.

When I asked to speak to my great grandmother May, Sofi informed that she was not available. She was already reborn. I asked if I know her or will know her again in this lifetime. My great grandmother May is now one of my nieces born to my second younger brother.

My grandfather Frank, Grandma Gerry's husband, was, along with my Grandma Gerry, one of my favorite people. Throughout my childhood and young adult life they were the only two family members from whom I had ever felt any real love. Sofi informed me that he was not available to speak with me.

"Is he a Spirit Guide or guiding on Earth", I asked.

"*No*", Sofi replied.

"He was reborn already?" I asked, eager to discover if I knew him in this life.

"*Yes*"

"Why did he chose to be reborn so soon?" I inquired, curious as to why he would not choose to stay on the Other Side for a longer period.

"*He didn't choose!*" Sofi quickly replied.

"Was he chosen?" I asked thinking the Council may have chosen him to be born for a specific purpose.

"*No*"

"He didn't commit suicide. Why did he not have a choice?" I was puzzled.

"*He murdered someone.*"

Sofi explained that if a person murders another person in this life they have no choice but to be reborn on Earth. They do not get to stay on the Other Side. Most Souls, in judging themselves, are so

124

disappointed with themselves if they had murdered someone in their previous life, that they quickly re-enter a new life with no time in-between. Most Souls have a contract before entering a physical life agreeing, at minimum, to just get through life without killing oneself or others.

Wow! Again I was speaking to my Spirit Guide, communicating to me through a girl who does not know anything about me. My client definitely did not know anything about my family, especially family members who have passed many years before these sessions; family members who have never lived in Florida. If this was not real could she not make up better reasons? Most reasons, for not being available, are very different.

∞

At the request of a high school friend, while communicating with my Spirit Guide through Page, I asked if she could locate a friend from junior high school who had passed away around a year or so ago. Sofi located her with no problem; the girl was still not adjusted to the Other-Side completely. The girl had left behind two children. Sofi, with this girl's Soul present on the Other-Side, explained that this girl actually had no connection with her two children. It was odd to me. However, Sofi explained to me that my friend's brief existence on Earth was for the learning experience of her husband and their two children she left behind. Sometimes individuals are born for the learning and growing of others.

Some entities, on the Other Side, choose to be born into a life with disabilities, and serious illnesses,

125

with no specific life goal or path of any kind. They choose to come into existence so that the people to whom they are born, family members, and all the people who ever come into contact with them, can learn and grow. Unfortunately, sometimes there is no growing for the parents. Sometimes the parents fail in working and growing through their path.

∞

Wanting information on the "rules", I asked, "So if you kill someone, you have no choice you have to be reborn?"

"*It depends.*" Sofi responded.

She explained, in depth, the difference between murdering and killing. Without going into too much detail there are infinite levels of killing with infinite levels of why. Murder basically comes down to a deliberate act not influenced by external forces, or internal interpretations of external forces. With infinite variations to the stimuli along with how one may process the stimuli, there are infinite ways in which one may be lead to kill or murder. In a physical life a person can examine themselves, their thoughts, the reasons, the causes, and the effects to attempt to justify their actions or not. However, when you are on the Other Side, you truly know your "INTENT" and you judge yourself. You absolutely know the difference between the infinite levels of killing and of murder.

At first I assumed that my grandfather did not forgive himself, perhaps, for killing people in the Korean War. I never heard that he killed anyone in the war. He was a driver, a transporter, but it still could have been possible. However, Sofi said it had nothing to do with the war. He had murdered someone.

Who did he kill? Why? What were the circumstances surrounding it? All questions I threw at her. She told me that he had killed someone as a favor for a friend. She would not tell me whom he had killed. However, she did tell me my grandfather's friend's name using the proper form of the name. Sofi used the proper name for people quite often, for example, she would say Peter for someone known as Pete. The name of the friend made sense. He was actually a Mafia captain for one the five families in New York City. My grandfather was not a made member of any crime family, as far as I knew, but this person, and all of his associates treated my grandfather with much respect. Again, it was impossible for my client to know this information.

She went on to tell me that he did not get to spend much time on the Other Side. He was on a lower level of the Other Side, while his new life was mapped out. She told me, at the time, he was already a three-year-old girl living on Earth. He was reborn to face the same situations and circumstances that he faced in his previous life. Sofi also informed me that I will meet him/her in this lifetime. I did not ask at the time, but I am hoping he/she comes to my 2-Day Healing Workshop to wipe away all negative Karma with absolute forgiveness and we can bring her to walk along a higher path. I want everyone to get out of their own way, to evolve their Souls' to the highest levels, to be aware of their true Infinite and Eternal nature.   Maybe my grandfather, as a girl in this lifetime, will read this book and decide to visit the Other Side and gain absolute knowledge and awareness.

Curious about the "rules", I inquired for clarifications.   Sofi, as well as Sheena, informed me that suicide was, besides murder, against the 'rules'. They instructed me that if a human on Earth commits suicide, even though we judge ourselves, they have no choice and are reborn quickly, sometimes, instantly, without getting to enter the higher areas of the Other Side.   Sofi said that the minimum we have to do in this life is to just get through each life.

Even though this information is coming from above, I disagree.   I am an absolute firm believer in the Infinite.   There are infinite possibilities!   Not every person who commits suicide is reborn immediately with no choice.   In bringing countless people to the Other-Side to communicate with loved ones and Spirit Guides I have received a plethora of valuable information.

Communicating with individuals who have committed suicide is also possible.   I have had clients on the Other-Side communicating directly with loved ones who had passed by their own hands.   Some had to do extra work to get to a certain level, or frequency, to move higher, but they had the choice to stay on the Other-Side.   They were able to learn and grow, and to continue evolving their Soul on the Other Side with the option to eventually be reborn on Earth.   Being reborn, however, was not mandatory.

There are so many paths, with numerous sub-paths, for Souls to take in the physical world. Some entities are born with a path to commit suicide, not for their purpose or evolvement, but to provide a lesson for someone else. Perhaps it was necessary in the evolvement of family members, and friends, of the individual who commits suicide - how they deal with it, how they adjust in life with their reactions, responses, and overall effects.

Sometimes an entity was scheduled to depart earth around a certain time and that time had passed. Time lines and realities shift constantly. It was their time, and things came into play in their life that brought them to suicide. Other times there are powerful negative influences that actually 'force' certain individuals to commit suicide. As I mentioned earlier there are the possibilities of attachments; discarnate spirits who have not crossed over and who are in 'spiritual pain'. These attachments sometimes influence depressed states that can be unbearable for the person. When attachments enter a person, especially one that was not meant to experience such pain, the hopelessness and numerous negative feelings, emotions, and thoughts take over. These individuals take their own life, but are not accountable for this action. Sometimes these attachments, not only influence the person to take their own life, but actually force them to do it.

Those who are addicted to drugs and overdose, whether deliberate or not, still have a choice to be reborn. Of course, they will judge themselves, and most are disappointed how they handled their life, even when the most horrible atrocities had happened to them, pushing them into drug addiction, and they will choose to be reborn on Earth to experience a similar life with similar choices. They do have a choice to stay on the Other-Side, for as long as they like, to learn and grow, and to build up energy, strength, and higher frequencies, to do a better job in their next physical life. Therefore, if someone you know had committed suicide it is still very possible that they are enjoying themselves, free of pain, on the Other-Side and they may very well be available for you to visit.

When asking a Spirit Guide questions, many times, you have to ask specific questions with no variations. They can be very literal. And you have to make sure you ask one question at a time, mostly, because they may just answer the last one. When I asked the question about the 'rules' and was told that suicide was a "no no" they did not elaborate. Something can be against the rules, but there can also be numerous factors to determine if the rule was actually broken. So, I will just say, at this time, if there is an uncertainty, follow the rule: all you have to do, is to just get through life without murdering someone and without taking your own life. And even if a loved one had taken their own life it does not necessarily mean that they have been reborn. The loved one may be available on the Other Side waiting to communicate with you.

Another note I should mention: sometimes a Spirit Guide will give you certain information, that may change later, but you needed to hear it a certain way at the time you were told for yourself, your highest good, for guidance in a certain way. Maybe I went into depth about suicide so much because I needed to hear it at the time. I truly do not want one person on this planet to ever suffer even a little bit, let alone so much that they would consider suicide. I am a healer and when I heard it was against the 'rules' it pushed me even harder to make sure I heal as many people as possible.

∞

My goal is for any person who comes into my path to never suffer again, on any level, with anything. There is no reason for it. Even if you chose to come to earth to experience the toughest life, most severe trauma, to experience the worst pain and loss, it does not mean you have to suffer your whole life. Yes, you may come into this life to experience the negative, but most importantly, you came into this life to overcome the negative. You are here to transcend this physical reality, to remember who you really are, where you came from, and where you will return. You are an amazing and powerful eternal being of light!

As I stated earlier Page came back several times for me to speak directly to my Spirit Guide and to speak to others' Guides. I have dozens of video recordings of our sessions. When she visited I would speak to my Spirit Guide for three hours at a time; receiving so much information about this life, the life after, eternity, and the Infinite.

As you continue to read, hopefully you are at the point of being more than just open to the possibility of life after death. Hopefully you accept that once you, or a loved one, leave this life it is not the end. Maybe you are beginning to be more aware of the fact that you are eternal because the more you realize, perhaps, you would like to experience the Other-Side now.

The conversations with my Spirit Guide channeled through Page - the knowledge, the wisdom, and much of that information will be described throughout the remainder of the book. I am confident that even the toughest skeptics are beginning to open up because there is just so much happening with my interactions, and guiding clients and students to the higher realms, to the Other Side that they realize they cannot refute it. There is too much to be left just to coincidence or just "imagination".

My interactions with my own Spirit Guide through Page, a sixteen-year-old girl who never knew me or anything about me, was absolute proof of the existence of the Other Side. If I had been at an eighty percent up to ninety seven percent certainty of the Other Side before these sessions; I was now at the one hundred percent point of certainty. The sessions with Page channeling my Spirit Guide allowed me to be absolutely certain of the reality of our true infinite and eternal Souls.

Hopefully, whatever level of certainty you may have had before reading this book has now increased. I will reveal more to you to break down any obstacles you may still have, if any, bringing you as close to the one hundred percent point as possible. Perhaps, by the time you finish reading this book you will not only be open, but absolutely eager to experience the Other Side for yourself - giving you a beautiful and peaceful state of Knowing with ABSOLUTE CERTAINTY!

CHAPTER 8: CHANNELING

"My Soul is from elsewhere, I'm sure of that, and I intend to end up there."
- Rumi

"You deserve to be loved perfectly, and to share love perfectly."
- Geozuwa

During one of her return visits, to communicate with my Spirit Guide, after guiding Page into the deepest states of hypnosis, separating her mind from her body, and bringing her to the Other Side, we discovered that Sofi was not available. Page was on the Other Side with many entities present; I directed her to become aware of Sofi. Instead another entity, a male, came forward to tell her that Sofi was not available.

This male entity informed her that he was also my Spirit Guide. His name was Vic. He was actually a supervising Guide in charge of Spirit Guides who were guiding several people alive on Earth. He agreed to enter the girl to communicate with me directly. Upon entry, he began to answer the many questions I presented. Sofi was not available because she was called to meet with the council. The council was reviewing her future life's blueprint.

Sofi had been my Spirit Guide even before this life. She was a very old Soul, Vic explained, but she was never born on earth. Most people assume or are mis-taught that an old Soul has had many reincarnations on earth. Vic explained that there are higher evolved, old Souls, being born for the first time in our current lifetime. She never had a "physical" life, but she was a very evolved Soul. And the Council had chosen her to be born, for the very first time, to me. That was pretty exciting news! Not only did I have the opportunity to communicate with my Spirit Guide, but she was going to be my daughter! According to Vic, she was going to be born to me as one half of a set of twins. Her twin brother was not yet chosen, however.

Vic informed me that he had taken a more active role, with me, a few times during my life. He occasionally stepped in, instead of Sofi, to help me, guide me, or give me signs. Sofi, at the time, was unable to move, shift or alter, physical matter. Vic, being of a 'higher power' as he explained it, was quite adept at it. He would change or move the physical to communicate with the humans under the Guides he was charged with, when necessary.

He described a few occasions in which he had done this with me to give me messages or get my attention. He explained that he actually entered the animals who had given me messages in the past. Vic also mentioned a time in Atlantic City when I was in a No Limit Texas Holdem Poker tournament. Of course, just to illuminate, again, the girl sitting in the recliner had no idea about me or who I am. She definitely, could not possibly have known about the times and locations of specific events in my life, let alone,

135

supernatural phenomena on those dates at those locations.

The poker tournament was very interesting to me because of what I experienced at the time. I never knew what it meant, if anything. I was sitting at the poker table with a minimal amount of chips left. As the second card was being dealt to me, it appeared as though the entire room was shaking. There was a loud frequency similar to a sonic boom sounding like a crisp loose-leaf paper being crumpled, that filled the entire room. At the same time as the noise was occurring the table was shaking as if we were in the middle of an earthquake. The duration of this event was a mere few seconds, but really startled me. I was looking around to discover that no one else was affected.

As I looked around my table, everyone had a poker face, and it was surprising to me that no one was even slightly rattled. I assumed that since it felt like we were in the middle of an earthquake, combined with the shaking and the accompanying sounds, there would be more reactions from the people around me. I asked a few people at the table if they felt the entire room shaking, or at least the table. Confused, I also asked if anyone heard the noises. No one had. I looked at my cards - they were pocket aces! My cards, were aces, and combined with what just happened physically, visually, and auditorily, I knew something just happened out of the ordinary. I tripled up winning the hand. Unfortunately, I did not win that particular tournament.

Vic told me that he had caused that event that no one else noticed. He explained to me that he changed my cards to aces to relay a personal message to me, and that things were about to change. When he told me what my original cards were I wanted to know specifically, down to the suits of each card. My original cards were the King of diamonds and the Jack of spades.

Shortly after, when I was in New York City, I had a client who wanted to go to the Other Side for information from her Spirit Guide. When I invited her Spirit Guide to come in, he did; however, the client would not let go completely. She was actually on the Other-Side, sitting on a bench with a loved one who had passed, but was too curious about the information from her Spirit Guide. The woman was capable of being a full channel, like Page, by not being in her physical body the entire time of the experience. When I do these types of sessions I have the client write down a list of questions especially if I plan to have the Spirit Guide enter. She wanted to know the answers, so she kept popping back in. The Spirit Guide did say she was interfering a bit with the process because some of the answers were what she hoped for instead of what they actually were.

Since she was interfering a bit, I asked her Guide, who had already relayed that she was familiar with me and all of my Guides, to call on Vic. I asked the Guide to ask Vic about the Atlantic City 'event' in which he did 'something' to get my attention. I did this because I wanted to confirm that I could still get information of value for the client.

Her Spirit Guide, inside the woman, told me that Vic altered the physical and that is why I experienced the sounds and the table shaking. I pushed the Guide for more by asking, "What in the physical did Vic alter?"

From the woman's body, her guide replied, *"He changed your cards to Aces."*

Now more excited with this level of confirmation, I continued to ask, "What were the original cards?"

"King of diamonds and Jack of spades." – Was the response.

Upon hearing the confirmation of the two original cards I was overwhelmed with feelings of joy. I sat for a moment and smiled. I was smiling with gratitude for knowing how wonderful and amazing all of this is. We are truly infinite and eternal beings. Anything and everything is absolutely possible!

The session with this woman was one of the earlier channeling sessions in my career. I was just beginning to have a channeling session option available for all clients. And for me, this was another confirmation of a beautiful connected world from which we all come, and to which we are all returning. We have Spirit Guides, who love us, help us, and guide us to navigate the paths we choose, or the paths we were chosen to follow. They help us accomplish our life's goal, our life's purpose. What would the changing of my cards do to help me along my path? Putting aside the personal message that I received, it showed me so much on so many levels: that anything and everything is possible, and we are not alone. We are never alone in our struggles and pain, even if it seems that way, we have amazing higher evolved entities - always there for support and love!

After the session with the New York City client, of course, I had many more questions for Sofi upon my return to Florida. During the next session with Page, Sofi explained that the client had been too interested in the answers to her questions and so she had interfered with the channeling. Because she was not interested in the answers to my personal questions – not being related to her directly, she let go, enough, at those points. And this brought us into our discussion on channeling.

∞

There are many levels to channeling. Some would consider the sessions I have done with clients before Sofi as a form of channeling, because the clients were receiving messages and information from beyond. Many mediums, real ones, do receive messages from the Other Side, channel, and then relay it to the client. I prefer to bring the client directly to the Other Side to experience and learn firsthand. However, I do not include those sessions in my definition of channeling. Nor do I include channeling various energies such as the awareness of the Sun, the Earth, or stars. For the purposes of this book and this chapter I am referring to the channeling of specific entities in my definition. Also, the people who have attachments are not channeling. Attached entities, sometimes thousands of attached entities, "share" a physical body space. Even if they have the permission of the host, this is unhealthy and, most of the time, very damaging for all involved.

When I am speaking of channeling I am referring to the infinite levels of partial and complete channeling of specific positive, highly evolved entities, which I will now describe. The sixteen-year-old girl, Page, who allowed my Spirit Guides to enter her physical body to communicate with me directly, is a full channel. The girl was no longer in her body when I was communicating with my Spirit Guides. There was absolutely no interference and my Guides easily use her physical body, temporarily, to impart valuable information.

This complete channeling is very healthy; as a matter of fact, it is extremely healing on many levels. The girl's mind and Soul are reenergized and healed with all of the Pure Love Energy by being on the Other Side during the process. She receives valuable knowledge and information, even if not readily available to her conscious awareness. And all of this Loving, healing, energy is brought back to the physical. In addition, having the Guide, a highly evolved entity with natural healing energy emanating from the Source of all creation, channeled - gives the physical body all of the healing that is needed. Depending on the client, or student, I will use this method to effectively and completely heal the individual.

At first I assumed everyone could fully channel. After trial and error I discovered that this is not the case. Sofi educated me on some of the various levels and requirements of channeling. Page was able to channel because, according to Sofi, she was of a higher power. That meant she had a more evolved Soul and her energy vibrated on a higher frequency to allow Spirit Guides to enter. Sofi continued to inform me that Page developed channeling skills in previous lifetimes and continued to train on the Other Side between her physical lives.

Spirit Guides also go through training to be able to be channeled by people living on Earth. This specialized training, on the Other Side, is one of the infinite learning and growing that takes place. They also practice to slow down their energy and frequencies to communicate in various ways on infinite levels with humans. Spirit Guides also must train in languages and learn the limitations of current human understanding. On the Other Side there is no need for verbal communication and all entities understand one another regardless of the languages spoken. The intention and frequencies of thought are all that is required on the Other Side to communicate with each entity's awareness.

∞

Inquiring about my abilities to channel, Sofi not only gave an affirmative response, but she claimed that I had channeled several times throughout my life. At first I was not consciously aware of, or did not entirely remember certain experiences, I wanted some examples.

Sofi asked me if I remember the time I was driving on the Staten Island Expressway in my late teens on my way to Brooklyn. She was referring to a moment when I was driving on the highway and it was twelve noon as I was passing exit thirteen. It felt as though I had just blinked my eyes, with a brief moment of nausea, when I looked down at the clock again and it was 3:30 p.m.! It was 3:30 p.m. and I was just passing exit 13. At the time I was so confused feeling all sorts of weirdness. Over three hours had passed and I was in the same location driving! I brushed it off, knowing I could not discuss it with anyone, because of what people might think. With my Spirit Guide Sofi, channeled through Page, she brought up that very moment that I had never divulged to anyone!

Sofi told me that at that very moment I was immediately called to the Council and Vic had entered my physical body. In my meeting with the Council we discussed certain shifts in time lines and realities, as described to me by Sofi because I was not consciously aware of that meeting. As she was telling me of this event I could not dispute it, instead, I continued to listen in awe. Sofi was confirming a real event in my physical life of which I had never known the meaning, or the reality. She continued to inform me that the three hour chunk of lost time was because my awareness had just shifted into a new time line. The new time line was necessary for me to have my physical life learn lessons that were not going to come to my awareness in the previous time line.

Moreover, Sofi informed that, according to Earth or human understanding, I was on the Other Side meeting with the Council and other beings, and Soul Circles, for a few months. Vic was inside of my

142

body the entire time! I am not sure what he was doing for a few months in that timeline and I did not think to ask. However, when I was sent back into my physical body it was a new time line, a different reality. Another reason, brought to my attention, for the missing time was to have a focal point in that time line that can be revisited when needed.

∞

Hopefully I did not lose you with the last few paragraphs. What I just described sounds way out there, I know. However, I had never communicated with anyone about losing the three hours and about being in the same exact spot on the highway while driving. The explanation of this experience was imparted to me when I asked about my abilities to channel. Sofi, my Spirit Guide channeled through Page, explained the extraordinary details of the event of which I had not been consciously aware prior to that session. Depending on your level of awareness, your frequencies, and your evolvement, up to this point, as you are reading this for the first time, you are going to process it in a way that will be entirely different than others' who are reading this.

Time really is not what most humans think it is. This book is an introduction to the infinite, and an invitation to experience the Other Side with your current consciousness. Although this book is an introduction I will reiterate that anything and everything is absolutely possible and I will explain to you a little more about Time. On one level there is no such thing as time, and everything is right now. And there are infinite levels and angles of the now.

Depending on your perceptions of, or how you choose to perceive, time will be exactly how time will look, feel, and be created in this physical reality. Always remember that there are infinite possibilities. You can shift, alter, influence, and absolutely control time. You can, also, easily travel through and outside of time as well. I love teaching my students how to do so.

You can have simple time distortion in hypnosis with suggestion. You can be in hypnosis for three hours and it will feel as though you have only been in hypnosis for five minutes with or without suggestion - depending on the level of depth or height of your session. You have probably experienced times in which you were having so much fun and time flew by. Or you may have been sitting in a boring class and it felt like an eternity for one minute to pass by. You can switch that so it feels like time slows when you are having fun, to enjoy it more, and you can speed time up so that it feels like time flew even in the most boring circumstances.

Not only can you have your mind switch the feeling of time distortion for certain occasions, but you can shift all levels of 'actual' time with your mind and energy. I do shift time often. For instance, there was a time, when as a licensed builder years ago I would hire painting sub-contractors to paint the inside and outside of the new homes I was building. Each painting contractor was paid the same amount for the job regardless of how long it took or how many workers they had on the job. Sometimes it would take a couple of weeks even with a painting crew of six. The work that was done was not very good. So I decided to do the painting of my new construction homes myself.

After showing up at the home, before I began to paint, I would take a deep breathe, at the same time shift all energy with my mind intending with an absolute knowing, "I move fast, time moves slow". As I exhaled I visualized myself moving at top speed completing the entire home inside and out, and I felt the shift. The average size of these homes was about 2000 square feet. There were three bedrooms, two bathrooms, living room, dining room, kitchen, and two-car garage. I primed the exterior of the home, painted the cathedral and vaulted ceilings inside, prepped the walls, painted the entire exterior, painted the entire interior walls, doors, and molding. All of this was done in a few hours. What I did in a few hours a professional crew of six had difficulties completing in several full days. And I always received compliments on how well the painting was done with each home I personally completed.

Some of my students use this technique for all sorts of occasions. One of my students would have to get on the train at exactly eight a.m. to be in work by nine a.m. In the past, if she missed the eight a.m. train she would be late for work. After she attended my 2-Day Healing Workshop she was excited to let me know that there were a few times in which she, not only missed the eight a.m. train, but boarded trains well passed eight and still made it to work by nine. On at least one occasion she boarded a train at 8:45 a.m. and she walked into her place of employment at 8:55 a.m.

As long as you believe it, expect it, and know it - everything works! Depending on what level you are on, you will probably begin to dabble with time shifting. When you intend to shift time, with, "I move fast, time moves slow", know that you are doing so and it will work wonderfully. Believe, expect, and most importantly - KNOW! Also, when you use this technique make sure you are only intending it for certain situations to accomplish specific tasks.

There have been a number of clients with whom I have had unexpected time shifts during the hypnosis sessions. For example, a three hour session with one client was already expired, but because I was not finished with the suggestions he required, I continued until twenty minutes passed the allotted time. As I emerged him from hypnosis there was a shift in time that we both felt. When he emerged, instead of being over twenty minutes, we still had twenty-five minutes remaining. Maybe doubters would say that the time was noticed wrong - it was not. So I will describe another session with you. And keep in mind I had several such sessions with big shifts in time.

I was doing a dream control hypnosis session with my wife on December 21, 2012. We began the session at nine p.m., both of us noticing the time because we are usually sleeping by ten p.m. We knew it was going to be a long session and that was why the time had been important to us. The session was going passed 10, 10:30, and 11:30 - I was frequently checking the time as I was guiding her through the dream state to accomplish specific goals for herself and the both of us. I was finally emerging her from the three hour session, both of us feeling all of the adjustments that were made during the dream control session, as it was turning midnight. We were both completely amazed when we discovered that the time was nine p.m. We made sure we checked every clock, computer, and cell phone to confirm that the time was in fact nine p.m. It was!

∞

One of the issues for adults with channeling is their inability to let go. Regardless of what state of hypnosis they are in when it comes time to channel, they automatically bring their conscious mind back to the forefront, thus interfering with the entire process. They are so eager to experience it they will not let go. Even the full channels, many times, will not let go enough to completely channel, but only partially channel.

Besides taking clients and students to the Other Side to communicate with their loved ones, their Spirit Guides, to learn and grow, to heal I also do channeling sessions. These sessions are done for various purposes including, healing, gaining knowledge wisdom, and having fun. From time to time I will also conduct Channeling Training Workshops. In these workshops the students discover if they are, at that moment in time, full channels. They also discover, from their Spirit Guides, if they are not, whether they will be able to fully channel in this lifetime. Usually everyone can be guided to do so in this lifetime.

In a recent Master Healer's class I was teaching in New York City for graduates from both my 2-Day Healing Workshop and my Hypnosis/NLP Certification course I did a channeling session with one of my students to illustrate how channeling can be used for powerful healing. When the student's Spirit Guide initially entered, the student was still in his body, off to the back. The Spirit Guide informed me that the student did not leave his body because he had too much fear from his up-bringing and childhood. I immediately asked his Guide if it would be ok to heal whatever it was that he had experienced in his childhood and everything associated with his up-bringing - all the causes and effects. His Spirit Guide agreed to heal the student on every level - emotional, psychological, energetic, spiritual, cellular, molecular, physical, and more. And as the Spirit Guide was healing the student on every level necessary, I too was healing the student, and removing any darkness from, wherever it was needed.

We discovered that in the process of healing what was needed, the student allowed himself to be a full channel. The student was only aware of the first few moments of his Spirit Guide entering his body while they were sharing space. That channeling session was over an hour long. Although he was fearful in the beginning, his Spirit Guide and I were able to eliminate that fear and heal him on many levels - and he was now a full channel. All of the students in the workshop were in awe during the whole process. They were able to see and feel all of the shifts in energy around him and in him. When he appeared the next morning in the classroom he was full of life and completely healed.

When I do these sessions, as with Page, I have the client/student in the higher states of awareness, on the Other Side, and I invite their Spirit Guide to come in. Many times the client will display the same physical signs of the guide entering the physical body as Page. The Guide will let me know when they are in by saying "Hello". Then, I check to see if the client/student is still present.

If the person is still present I find out in what capacity. There are infinite levels of partial channeling. Sometimes the guide will let me know that the client is still present in the physical and able to observe, but not interact - unlike Page who is absolutely not present in the physical and whose awareness and energy is on the Other Side during the session. On some occasions the Spirit Guide comes in, and the client is "off to the back", as they describe it, and still able to interact without interfering in the process. Sometimes they describe, in real time, that the client is off to the side and still able to interact without interference. Usually, however, in the situations in which the client is off to the back, or the side, it is the Guide that does all of the communicating during the session. Other times the Spirit Guide is in, but the client speaks, relaying all of the information from the particular Guide who is present. I have, also, during Channeling Workshops, had students Channel more than one Spirit Guide at the same time.

Besides gaining valuable information and knowledge from the Spirit Guides during channeling, the client/student gains so much awareness, and healing. Much of the awareness received is that of Infinite possibilities, the eternal energy, life, Pure Love, understanding, and peace. They know this world is temporary and we have a beautiful eternity to look forward to. The healing, without being guided, takes place just by having the Spirit Guide, higher evolved entity, enter the physical body. The higher energy, frequencies, vibrations, and pure love of your Spirit Guide automatically increases your energies, cells, and DNA, to adjust to love, forgiveness, and perfection - allowing the healing to take place, sometimes instantly.

Anyone experiencing or witnessing channeling sessions, even if they did not previously believe in the Other Side, strongly believe afterward! One of my friends in Florida was not sure if any of this were real, never having experienced it. He was only aware of what he had been taught or told by his parents and church goers. When he described to his wife what I was doing, she adamantly said that it was just the girl's imagination. She exclaimed that it was not real.

Luckily for my friend he was more open to the possibility due to my confidence and the matter-of-fact way I spoke about the Other Side. He ignored his wife's ridicule about what I do. He knew me in a social context of having fun with never anything serious, until the Other Side was brought up in a conversation.

I do not go around speaking about the Other Side or preaching. We all have our own paths, our own belief systems, and although a part of my path is to bring awareness of the Other Side and our Infinite possibilities I do not, just go around speaking about it. Some people are so entrenched in their beliefs, and limitations, that if anything, even slightly, confronts their belief system, they are brought to such anger. For instance, everyone in my family has asthma - on both my mother's side and my biological father's side. I, too, was born with asthma. When I was in school, four or five years old, and was prohibited from participating in Gym class, because of the asthma, I decided I did not want it! I never had it again! It was gone!

Countless clients, whether in private sessions, group sessions, or my workshops, completely eliminate asthma in one session or one day. People suffering their entire lives with asthma, after the first day of my 2-Day Healing Workshop are completely cured. It is absolutely eliminated and it never returns! When I explained this to my aunts and cousins at a family gathering, the last one I attended, they all became angry; one aunt was on the verge of violence! The one I spoke of in Chapter five, and yes this was the same family gathering which ended up being my last. While inhaling the asthma pump she yelled at me that it is impossible to get rid of asthma through hypnosis. She was yelling at me about how real asthma was. She completely ignored and refused to believe the countless testimonials of clients and students with whom I have worked to permanently, often instantly, eliminate asthma. Without going through the entire story again I think you have enough of the picture. I was not trying to convince anyone - I just merely offered a session to get rid of asthma.

Back to my friend in Florida; he had met Page and was familiar with how she spoke, and how she behaved. His perception of her was that of a typical tough, 'gangsta' type teenager. When he learned that she was channeling my Spirit Guides he wanted to see. First, he watched a video of one of my sessions with Page. His interest, and belief, heightened. He watched the process of how I separated her mind from her body, guiding her awareness to the higher levels, to the Other Side, and then to have my Spirit Guide enter. He watched intently the physical signs of my Guide entering her body, replacing her in the physical.

My friend was convinced that Page was no longer in her body. He confirmed that the voice and tone were different. "She" used words and phrases that he knew that Page could never have known. When he ran into Page again, he even asked her about certain words, confirming that she indeed did not know any of the meanings, and during their conversation she looked at him as if he were crazy. Page had never watched herself on the videos of the channeling sessions.

My friend was, perhaps, at the time, a little fearful or worried about what his wife would say, if he himself tried to channel. However, he did want to communicate with his Spirit Guide. He had questions. So we set it up for Page to do a session with my friend present. When she was on the Other Side her Spirit Guide, Sheena, was present. I decided to have her Guide come in first. Sheena said that she was familiar with my friend and his Spirit Guides. After asking if one were available to speak with us, she confirmed that he was present, but Sheena told us that his Spirit Guide would not be able to come in to speak with us. His Guide never trained to be able to enter a physical body alive on earth. Sheena assured us that we could ask our questions about my friend's life and path and that she would relay the answers. We discovered that his Spirit Guide was his Guide through many lifetimes and had intimate knowledge of everything about him. All of his questions were answered. My friend was content, in awe, grateful, and, now, a firm believer in how real it was. He was absolutely convinced of a life after death!

∞

Although I could guide you to channel you probably do not have to channel to believe in the Other Side. You do not have to shift time or even believe that you can, but hopefully you are open to it being absolutely possible as with other metaphysical possibilities. If you were not convinced earlier, perhaps through your reading of these accounts you are convinced to the absolute reality of life after death. If you already believed and had faith that your Soul is eternal prior to reading this book, I am certain that belief and faith has been strengthened by now. Perhaps you are also developing a view that is not limited by any physical restraints.

The accounts of my students and clients are of regular everyday people; some with really tough and difficult lives, others with lives just as regular as your neighbors. These individuals were not raised and trained in metaphysics. Many of my clients' belief systems did not include anything other than this physical reality. Many clients, prior to meeting me, believed once you die you no longer exist. Now they have an absolute knowing, an absolute awareness, of the reality of the Other Side because they allowed me to guide them there. They received valuable information, knowledge, and healing that many would consider miraculous. These regular everyday people now have a new outlook on this life - they have answers, and they know with absolute certainty that our Souls are eternal and continue to live after this life ends.

CHAPTER 9: BENEFITS of VISITING the OTHER-SIDE

"There are only two ways to live your life. One is as though nothing is a miracle. The other is as though everything is a miracle."

-
                                                    Albert Einstein

"Allow yourself to walk along a higher path of Love, Light, and Happiness."

                                                    -Geozuwa

You may have read accounts of people who have had near death experiences. They may describe their experience of entering the Other Side. These individuals also report coming back to their bodies, returning with remarkable gifts, insights, healed, and awesome abilities. I am here to tell you that you do not have to die to visit the Other Side! You do not have to have a near death experience to gain amazing awareness, insight, beautiful gifts, healing, knowledge, metaphysical skills and extraordinary abilities. You can have all of it now!

One obvious benefit of visiting the Other Side, now, in your current consciousness, is, of course, closure. Maybe you were not afforded the opportunity to say goodbye to a dying loved one. Perhaps you want to share the feelings you did not have a chance to share when they were alive. Do you want to know why a particular loved one treated you the way they did?　Perhaps you are seeking forgiveness for an offense committed to a loved one, or you are wishing to let your loved one know you have forgiven them. Imagine embracing your loved ones after they are gone. Imagine speaking to them directly in an area of Pure Love, positive energy, a beautiful place of complete happiness and joy.　There are so many benefits when you visit the Other Side.　To start with, you gain a peaceful closure, and absolute freedom from -, any type of depression, guilt, shame, anger, confusion, and fears.　There is no longer any fear of dying. You have an absolute awareness of where you are going when you leave this world.　You know with absolute certainty that you are an infinite and eternal being!

Another benefit is to have all of your questions, about your life, your path, your purpose, your future, answered!　When you visit the Other Side you are face to face with your Spirit Guides.　Your Spirit Guides, aka Guardian Angels, have an intimate knowledge of everything about you and your path. Are you at a cross road in your life?　Do you need to know which direction to take?　Are you overwhelmed with your current situation?　Are you on your correct path?　How many previous lives have you had?　Are you traveling through lifetimes with friends and families, and changing roles?　Is this person the right person for you?　Do you have a Soul Mate?　Will you be with your Soul Mate in this lifetime?　Should you accept the job offer?　Are you making the right decision? What is the best solution? Help!!!

Visiting with your Spirit Guides on the Other Side will give you invaluable information, answers, and guidance. Discover which way to go. Learn why certain people in your life did the things they did or why certain situations had to happen or did not have to happen. Discover your purpose! Learn if you are on your correct path and how to stay on it in a more positive way. Find out who your Soul Mate is and if and when you will meet. Become aware of what your future holds!

Yes, you will receive, firsthand, the answers to all of your questions. Your future will clearly be revealed to you. However, regardless of what your future is or supposed to be there are always infinite possibilities. If a thousand psychics, even your Spirit Guides, tell you the same information about your future, remember, nothing is written in stone! Or nothing has to be written in stone. You have the ability to change your future at any time, in an instant. With a simple thought, or in changing a certain belief system, you can change your future.

You are an absolute creator! Create your future exactly how you want it to be. Choose to be who you want to be. You do not have to continue through this life based on your experiences and what others say how you should. Do not accept anything less than your perfection.

∞

However, "stuff" does happen! There are billions of people on the planet. Each person creating reality. Sometimes there are interference patterns affecting your particular path unintentionally,

157

sometimes intentionally. Your thoughts and intentions combined with the thoughts and intentions of others' can create situations that can alter your future. Sometimes being followed by our Spirit Guides from the Other Side these interferences are observed and they must act to correct or at least alter, sometimes several life paths, to create new paths.

My friend Barry's wife, Doreen, wanted to do a channeling session for answers to her questions. She was able to partially channel. Doreen was the one using her vocal chords, not her guide, although he was present in her body. She discovered that her husband was not her Soul Mate, but was chosen to be her husband in this life by her actual Soul Mate and Soul family. Receiving this information I was thinking to myself they chose right, because he is probably the only person on Earth who could possibly deal with her. This was thought, of course, in the most loving way.

Doreen continued to relay information to me about her two children. She said that they were my close friends on the Other Side. One of her big questions was whether she would have more children or not. Many psychics and 'mediums' had told her that she would only have two children. Communicating with her Spirit Guide directly, for the first time, he, also, informed her that she was only having the two children she already had. It is not in her path to have any more children. She also stated that we were brother and sister in our last life before this one. Interesting, I felt a connection with her children, but I never had that feeling about her. So I enquired further of our past life together. Her Guide told her I had been a priest in Brazil. Not mentioning anything to her, I was already thinking about questioning my Spirit Guide through Page when I was back in Florida. Because I never had a feeling that we were related in a previous life, and because she did not fully channel her Spirit Guide, I was a little concerned that she was perhaps interfering.

I had never asked my Guides about my past lives before. I never asked about who I may be traveling with, or what I did in my previous life either. Concerning my past-lives the only information discussed to that point was that I had only one previous life on Earth and that this life is my last one on Earth. The next time Page channeled for me I asked my Spirit Guide if Page knew me before this life. Sofi told me that Page was my nephew in my last life.

"Was her father my brother or was her mother my sister?" I continued with my questions.

"His mother was your sister." Sofi replied.

"Do I know this woman in this lifetime?"

"Yes."

"Who is she?" I asked excited that I would be able to know who I know in this life was my sister in the previous life.

"Doreen."

"Doreen, Barry's wife?" I asked with amazement and excitement, for this was yet another confirmation of the reality of life after death.

"Yes."

I must point out that Doreen and Page had never met. They have no idea about one another. They have no connection in this life. Doreen lives in New York City. Page lived in Florida. So I was even more intrigued to continue with my questions and confirmations. And the confirmations continued to flow. Sofi told me that I was a priest and we lived in Brazil - more absolute confirmation of how real life after death is and how our Souls are Eternal. Wow!

∞

When I was at the National Guild of Hypnotists' annual conference in Massachusetts shortly after the sessions with Doreen and Sofi, through Page, I went to a workshop with Ramona Garcia and Marlene Mercedes. They are both adorable hypnotists who also happen to be highly talented psychics. Without going into detail about the personal messages with the abundance of confirmations they discussed with me for an hour and a half after their workshop had ended, they gave me an additional message pertaining to the previous paragraph. As Ramona was speaking to me about what Sofi originally revealed to me about who I am and what I was chosen to do, Marlene interrupted by saying, "Brazil. You were a priest in Brazil in your previous life." Ramona and I were speaking about my Soul Mate and the moment she would be entering my life when Marlene told me that. I did not say anything to either of them about the two channeling sessions, which had taken place shortly before the conference about previous lives. Then, Marlene stated, "You needed to hear that for you to trust in what your Spirit

Guides, and Ramona, are telling you. That is another confirmation".

∞

One afternoon, in Florida, I placed myself in a trance and energetically left my body to go do my healing work. As I am flying from location to location of where I am needed a big thunderous voice echoed, *"Doreen is having your baby!"* This stunned me and completely threw me for a loop. I immediately snapped back into my body. I was confused. The voice and statement was loud and clear. It was a complete impossibility for her to have my child. We were never together and would never be together. It was a strange and unsettling experience that I could not shake off the entire day.

Later, in the evening of the same day, I received a most interesting, and even more confusing, phone call from Doreen. She called wanting to know what was going on. She was yelling that she was pregnant! Her Spirit Guide, and so many psychic mediums told her she was only having two children. She was pregnant with her third child! Doreen wanted to have another session to find out why, on my next trip to New York City. I kept my experience of the day to myself, by the way.

When I was back in New York City a few months later we had the next session. I was just as concerned and eager to do this session as she was, but for other reasons. In the very beginning of the session her Spirit Guide told her that she was pregnant with my child. OK What?!?!?!?! I screamed inside my head, but out loud - I calmly replied to this information, "Doreen, he is aware that we have never been together and never would be together? Isn't he? How is this possible?"

Doreen continued to explain in a much calmer state than me. She was in a higher, blissful, state of awareness. Her Spirit Guide was also present in her physical body at the same time which is so peaceful, tranquil, and loving. Her Guide explained that, although she was not meant to have another child in this lifetime, she was having one of the children who was supposed to be born to me. Her daughter is my spiritual child, who was supposed to be born to me, but because of certain shifts in reality the child had to be born at that time. I was not ready for her. I was not even in a relationship at the time. I had never confided with her about my experience before her phone call to me. As you can see, stuff happens and paths can change.

∞

Depending on the level, and training, of your Spirit Guides, they may have more access to records, knowledge and wisdom, from the entire Universe and other worlds. If gaining enlightenment and eternal wisdom is what interests you, visit the Other Side. The Akashic Records, containing all wisdom and recordings of everything that has been and will ever be. Please keep in mind there are infinite possibilities and you are an absolute creator. The Akashic records can be changed as well. Regardless of the level of evolvement of your Spirit Guides, if they do not have access to the knowledge you require, they can be directed to call on a higher evolved entity to access that knowledge.

Recently I had a client on the Other Side who just wanted to have the experience. While she was there with her Spirit Guides she was having her questions about her life answered. Surprisingly, she did not have many questions. We had extra time, even after I directed her, with the help of her Guides, to heal on an emotional level.

I had been bombarded with many "signs" for a few weeks, before this particular session, and did not have the time to 'connect' to receive the answers. So I figured I would ask a few of my own questions. I asked her to ask her Spirit Guides if they were familiar with me. And to my surprise she said her Guides did not know me. This was the first time - it was so surprising, because every Spirit Guide, even the loved ones of the clients on the Other Side, personally knew me on the Other Side or, at least, knew of me.

I always keep ego out of what I do. The reason I am explaining this to you at this point is because of how it may sound. You have not met me in person yet. When I state that everyone knows me, or knows of me on the Other Side, it is because of the work I am doing in this life and for other personal reasons. Everything I do, is done with pure positive intentions and integrity. I want every single person to never suffer with anything ever again. I want every single living creature and every single human to live in complete happiness with perfect health. Of course, we are all on different levels of awareness, and that is ok. I do not judge, and I hope for others not to judge in any capacity. Just because I may have certain abilities, and awareness, does not make me any better than anyone else. Regardless of what level of vibration, frequency, or evolvement of Soul - we are still on this planet in this human world experiencing the heaviness of this world and all of the negatives thrown our way. Regardless of what level we are on, we are still in this world together and we should be helping one another to see past our experiences and the limitations that others try to place on us. And although I have all of these metaphysical abilities I teach others how to have them and how to do the same. I do not keep these abilities, or knowledge for myself to be "above" anyone else. I truly want every person I teach to excel and to transcend, I truly want my students to do everything I can do and hopefully much more.

Many clients/students tell me during or after a session or workshop that, while on the Other Side, entities would appear to pass on greetings, gratitude, and love to me. It is a big part of my mission, my life's purpose, to bring awareness to the masses of the Other Side, of our infinite and eternal natures, so it does make sense that I would be known there. I am a Council member who has been chosen along with many other human beings alive today on this planet to assist and guide people to awaken to who they really are.

I asked my client to ask her Spirit Guides if they had access to the Akashic records. They did not. After asking her Guides to call upon a higher evolved entity who has access to the records one immediately appeared. This entity was aware of who I am. My client channeling, said that he was very excited to pass on a greeting to me. I asked this entity to access the records to see if I were still on track to open the Healing and Learning Center for Children. The client relayed that there were certain changes to that particular path, but that there would be several large donations which would allow it to materialize. When she emerged, she informed me that the entity, with the records access, was telling her, on the Other Side, of how important it is for me to build the center for children. She expressed to me that she felt so much gratitude from all of the energy around her when the center for children was mentioned.

∞

I will take a moment to share with you a little bit about the Healing and Learning Center for Children. Currently, in the United States there is an overwhelmed Foster Care system. Parents are not only failing to provide their children with the necessary nurturing, caring, protection, and love, but they are abusing and neglecting their children, many times in the worst nightmarish manner. Children are being removed from their home, the ones that get noticed, and are being placed in an overwhelmed, overcrowded foster care home. Sometimes these homes are even worse than the homes from which they are being removed.

Many of the children, unfortunately, grow up to continue the cycles of dysfunction and abuse that their families endured for generations. The Healing and Learning Center for Children will put an end to the cycles of dysfunction and abuse. Every child, from the earliest ages and at their own pace, will learn and master self-hypnosis. They will learn and use the most effective coping skills, through self-hypnosis, allowing them to be in control of how they feel, how they react and respond to the world, events, situations, and circumstances. They will have absolute respect for all living things, especially for themselves. They will know their true infinite potential. These children will never seek to manipulate, control, deceive, or take advantage of any other person in any form or capacity. They will grow knowing Pure Love and they will always have the most positive intentions for themselves and everyone else. They will move through life with strength, courage, confidence, clarity of mind, clarity of purpose, happiness and joy, with perfect health. They will have amazing skills to think for themselves. They will be raised with high and healthy self-esteem, self-worth, self-love and appreciation with confidence. These children will be raised with an absence of hate. They will grow with absolute respect combined with compassion, and love for all races, religions, colors, and all walks of life.

Some of you who read this may think that the learning center is an idealistic dream - not possible within this current reality. However, I know that, not only is it a realistic possibility, it is absolutely going to come into existence and spread. And many of you reading this already wish for, imagine, and know this Center to already be manifesting and materializing into existence. Think about how your life would be

166

different if you knew, as a child, everything that you know now, or will know in the future. Every child will be afforded the opportunity, at their own pace, to visit the Other Side. Imagine growing up knowing with absolute certainty that there is so much more to this world than what has been taught. Imagine growing up knowing with absolute certainty from where you come, where you are going, what your life's purpose is, which path to take, who your Soul Mate is, and how to prepare and grow through life. Imagine growing up communicating with your loved ones who have passed, and your Spirit Guides whenever you wish. Imagine knowing from the earliest ages of your true infinite and eternal nature, and your amazing ability to create the world around you. How wonderful it would be to KNOW from the earliest ages that your immune system is perfect and you remain healthy at all times. Also, knowing, if necessary, that you can heal yourself and others easily and powerfully. Imagine the amazing, peaceful, confident, happy, loving, healthy adults these children will become.

∞

There is actually much more, infinite, to the simple definitions given to Akashic Records. Going to the Other Side, visiting with your Spirit Guides, accessing the "Library of Knowledge", you can easily download, upload, infinite codes of information, knowledge and wisdom to your mind. Your awareness continues to increase exponentially when doing these types of sessions. I include a number of these sessions, combined with others, in my 2-Day Healing Workshop & Evolve Your Soul Training.

Before you come to the 2-Day Healing Workshop you will write out a list of all of the things you want to get rid of and wish to change about yourself. Bring a list of all of your goals, everything you want to accomplish, and who you want to be. All on the first day we get you out of your own way to realize your true infinite potential. You will have all negative thought patterns, and any negative energies permanently eliminated. You are brought to neutralize, let go, forgive, and overcome any negative experiences, traumas, and fears. This is part of the process to completely heal you of the causes and effects of all of your negative experiences. You learn self-hypnosis and several neuro-linguistic programming (NLP) techniques. At the end of the first day you are guided to the deepest states of hypnosis, your mind is separated from your body and guided to the higher states of awareness. Then from your mind, free of the physical, I guide you through that brilliant glowing tunnel to enter the Other Side to receive valuable information and knowledge about your life and your path from your Spirit Guides. Once there, the energy, the love, the frequencies, the amazing feelings of bliss, many times heal what needs to be healed instantly. Then I guide you even higher to connect to the center of the beautiful Pure Love White Light Healing Energy of God, the entire Universe, the Source of all Creation, and have you channel it through yourself to every person in the workshop.

Everyone is doing this at the same time from the center of Source while I continue to speak and guide the healing. My eyes are still open, but everyone disappears. All I see are various shades of purple mist. It feels as though I am walking on air while I enjoy the heat, the energy, the gratitude, the Love, and the healing that floods the room.

Many attendees, suffering their entire lives with asthma, allergies, diabetes, and so many other ailments, are completely healed! After the first day - vision is corrected, hearing is corrected, emotional, physical, and all levels of issues and pains are corrected and absolutely healed! On the 2nd Day I teach you how to connect to the beautiful Pure Love White Light Healing Energy of Source instantly through self-hypnosis to easily heal yourself and effortlessly heal others. You learn several techniques of remote healing to powerfully heal others regardless of the distance of time and space between you! You will absolutely be amazed at what you can do, what you can accomplish, and how wonderfully you feel! My students, using what they learn in this workshop, have gotten rid of death bed cancers, terminal liver disease, physical deformities, 'permanent' paralysis, and so much more!

Discover who your Soul Mate is! Learn if and when you will meet in this life. When asking your Spirit Guides the name of your Soul Mate, I have learned that we must be specific. Sometimes they give us the Soul's name of your Soul Mate which, in many cases, is different from their name on earth. So we ask for both names. Which of course, is a great opportunity to discover what your Soul's name is. Sometimes your current life's name is also your Soul's name. Sometimes a Vanessa will discover that her

Soul's name is Brian. Sometimes the Soul's name is an off-the-wall name like Azinkranthes. Sometimes the name of the Soul comes across as a sound, music, or frequencies that are interpreted in various ways.

When I have clients wishing to discover Soul Mate information, these sessions turn out dramatically different every time. Most people can live thousands of lifetimes without ever meeting their Soul Mate in the physical reality, even if they were meant to! There are rare occasions in which the Spirit Guides will not give the name on earth. Their reason is that they do not want to interfere with your path or the paths of the many people that could be shifted, because you have that information. If you are told that your Soul Mate's earthly name is Bob, you may not accept a date with a Gary - when it is quite possible that you would meet Bob through a date with Gary. It is also possible that Gary's birth name is Robert (Bob) - or Gary is the middle name of Bob which he prefers. There are infinite possibilities. If you interfere with your path in this manner, the Spirit Guides of all players involved have to work over time to get things back on track.

There have been clients who have come to me for their Soul Mate information to discover, while on the Other Side with their Spirit Guides that their Soul Mate is not even born in this life. I then direct them to visit with their Soul Mate on the Other Side. From then, usually, their Soul Mate agrees to assist their Spirit Guides in finding the right person, on Earth, for a perfect relationship. You do not have to be with your Soul Mate to have and maintain a beautiful, healthy, loving, perfect relationship. Sometimes clients discover that they have already met their Soul Mate in this lifetime. Soul Mates can enter your life as teachers, family members, and in all other forms. Clients have discovered that their worst enemy was their Soul Mate. In choosing paths and experiences for the future life, Soul Mates may have an agreement, not to be together romantically, but to help each other in the learning and growing process. Sometimes there is pain. And then there are other situations in which the client's Soul Mate is also their Spirit Guide.

Healing is another amazing benefit of visiting the Other Side. It is a beautiful place of Pure Love, forgiveness, and perfect healing. In doing a two hour workshop titled "Visit the Other Side" at the New Life Expo in New York City I had many people so grateful for the opportunity to visit with loved ones. There were also a number of people who eliminated issues they were suffering for their whole lives. One person described how, before he attended this mini-workshop, he was constantly in pain for decades. He would awake every morning, in unbearable pain, feeling as though he had been beaten with baseball bats throughout the entire night. The day after the workshop he awoke, for the first time in decades, with no pain whatsoever. He was absolutely amazed because all of his pain was completely gone! After a week, waking up refreshed, reenergized, happy, and pain free, he quickly signed up for my next 2-Day Healing Workshop. After attending the 2-Day Workshop he was no longer diabetic! The diabetes he had endured his entire life was gone and it never came back!

One gentleman attending the 2-Day Healing Workshop a few years ago was completely blind in one eye. He was blind in that eye for more than two decades. His other eye, although he could see through it, had constant black spots making it uncomfortable. In the middle of the first day, after one of our hypnosis sessions, he jumped up exclaiming, "I can see! I can see out of my eye!", as he was covering the other eye with his hand, proudly, excitedly, turning to everyone in the room, showing them he could now see. At the end of the first day there were no more black spots. He now has perfect vision!

Another gentleman, a very mechanical-world type with no exposure to the metaphysical and no spiritual background, was curious about my workshop, but was hesitant to attend. I decided to have him work the camera to video one of the workshops. He was absolutely blown away witnessing the transformations of the attendees just from the beginning of the first day to the end of the first day. After witnessing the second day and describing all of the energy he could feel and see by the end, he quickly signed up for the next workshop.

The day after the first day of the workshop in which he participated, he was sitting in his kitchen reading the newspaper. His wife walked in and he excitedly exclaimed to her, "Look I am reading the paper with no glasses! I don't need glasses anymore!" As he began reading sentences to her, she told him, because she did not believe that he could read without the glasses, that it was just in his mind.   His response, still with excitement, "Exactly!" He knew, from the workshop, the power of the mind. Although he had worn them his whole life, he no longer needed to wear glasses.   On the second day he was able to vividly see and feel auras!   He accepted the suggestions of perfect vision in every sense of the word and his third eye vision opened and expanded powerfully.   I then taught him how to turn that ability on and off on command.

Another benefit of visiting the Other Side is to connect to the Source of all Creation.   You can refer to this Source of Pure Love White Light as God, the Universe, whatever you wish, it does not matter.   But once you connect with Source, your awareness soars to levels you may have never dreamed possible.   You can become one with the entire Universe.   You feel the absolute connectedness of everyone and everything.   The benefits are too many to list when you reach this point and become one with God.   This is also a beautiful state to easily heal yourself and powerfully heal others.

You and everyone else, whether aware of it or not, constantly create the world around you.   When visiting the Other Side and connecting to Source, you increase your abilities to create reality to immeasurable heights.   Accessing the beautiful energy of pure creation allows you to easily and effortlessly manifest your intentions to materialize into this physical reality.   You begin to notice things falling into place exactly how you picture, imagine, and intend. Life and the energy around you begin to flow in the most positive way for your highest good and ultimate happiness.

In visiting the Other Side, your energies, your frequencies, and vibrations continue to increase and rise higher. Your awareness, on every level, continues to increase and expand. Your ability to create with your mind, your thoughts, your intentions, combined with the awareness, and the abilities to connect to Source continue to increase. One of the main reasons I do not advocate predicting the future is that I absolutely believe in you creating your future! There are no limitations! Do not accept anything that limits your dreams. As long as you do not try to control anyone else or their futures, take control of your life, and create! Of course, if you need answers and guidance, by all means, visit the Other Side to receive them. Also, by doing that, you will discover and become aware of your abilities to create. Furthermore, you can also ask, even command, your Spirit Guides to help you create and make things happen the way you want them to happen here on Earth. They are more than happy to oblige you and give you all of the assistance you need.

You do not have to die to experience the beautiful place to where you are going when you do pass from this world. You do not have to have a near death experience to receive powerful gifts and amazing abilities. You can visit the Other Side now and receive everything you need. An additional benefit, besides the new awareness and perspective of this life and who you are, is a new and amazing ability to have fun! Yes, you will absolutely allow yourself to enjoy life and all of your creations to the fullest! So how do you get there without dying?

CHAPTER 10: HOW to VISIT the OTHER-SIDE

"When the pupil is ready the teacher will appear."
- Unknown

"Everything can be so easy if you allow it to be. It is simple yet very powerful."

-Geozuwa

By now you are probably more interested in visiting the Other Side, especially after realizing that you do not have to die. There are several ways with your current consciousness, and awareness to get there. There are actually infinite ways, I, however, will list and describe a few that are available to you.

Meditation may afford you the opportunity. However, it is a method that can take a lifetime to achieve. Meditation is a very valuable tool and technique. However, most people will practice meditation every day for years, for decades, for an entire lifetime and still never reach the depths and heights that you will reach in one session of hypnosis. The main technique I use in which I bring you to the Other Side is with your mind through hypnosis. I guide you to the deepest states of hypnosis, separate your mind from your body, guide your mind to the highest states of awareness, and then I guide you through the brilliant glowing tunnel, coming from your mind, to the Other Side.

I also have a hypnosis CD series called the Inner Temple of Creation. I take you to the deepest states of hypnosis separate your mind from your body and then guide your mind, free of the physical, into the deepest areas of the infinite universe inside of you, to the tiniest most dynamic area of who you are. In this area everything is connected - you feel the oneness of the entire universe. I have Inner temple CDs for visiting with Spirit Guides, and visiting the Other Side. In the remote healing CD, currently exclusive for the attendees of the 2-Day Healing Workshop & Evolve Your Soul Training, I guide you, from your Inner Temple of Creation, to connect to Source to reenergize your Soul and every aspect of your being, then I guide you to heal others. I have countless accounts of students using this CD to do amazing, 'miraculous' healing.

Another favorite way in which you can reach the Other Side to have a beautiful experience is through astral travel. I have been energetically traveling outside of my physical body ever since I was a very young child. Through hypnosis I am able to teach and train others to easily separate their energetic body from their physical body in several different ways, to astral travel, and to remain consciously aware of the experience. I will usually use this method, if not done in private training sessions, in a follow up workshop to the 2-Day Healing Workshop & Evolve Your Soul Training, specifically for those who wish to astral travel to expand on their healing abilities.

Students, who have visited the Other Side through the methods of separating the mind from the body, explain how different the feelings, the sensations, the vision, and the awareness is when they enter the Other Side through the means of astral travel. One student believed that he was not having as vivid an experience as the other students in the Healing Workshop when guided to the Other Side. He enjoyed where he was, feeling all of the Pure Love and energy, during his first experience. He received answers to all of his questions and he was amazed with his increased awareness. However, this particular student was concerned that he did not see his Spirit Guides as clearly as his fellow students.

When he attended a follow up Astral Traveling Training Workshop his concerns quickly vanished. I directed him, from a heightened state of hypnosis, to energetically separate from his physical body. For him this was a much more sensory experience than when separating his mind from his body. The student loved that he could see his physical body in hypnosis sitting in the chair. Being able to see his energetic hands wave before his eyes allowed him to be even freer and expect much more with this awareness. He described to me that when I brought him to the Other Side through astral travel to meet with his Spirit Guides his experience was vastly different than the first session. Everything was clearer and brighter. Each session in guiding people to the Other Side is different with each person. Also, a person's experience can be vastly different on each occasion. Remember, each time you do this your awareness continues to increase exponentially, more so than the time before.

I have developed, and made available, several hypnosis CDs for astral traveling. In one of my dream control hypnosis CDs, after guiding you into a natural sleep, becoming aware that you are asleep, I then guide you to energetically leave your physical body. After noticing you are outside of, and seeing, your body sleeping, I direct you to re-enter your body to become familiar with the difference in the feelings and sensations. Then I guide you to, again, leave your physical body. You begin to energize your home, then I guide you to fly through your ceiling, through the clouds, out into the Universe to connect to the Source of all creation. After energizing every aspect of who you are in Pure Love you are then guided to astrally fly wherever you wish, to do whatever you would like to do.

Another method to visit the Other Side is through dream control. When you are lucid dreaming you have a different approach and have access to the infinite power of your mind. While you are in control of your dream, at any point you can command yourself or bring your awareness in any way that is most pleasing to you to the Other Side. I absolutely love teaching my students dream control. It is one of my favorites. So much can be done in the dream state. When you visit the Other Side, visiting with loved ones who have passed, visiting and communicating with your Spirit Guides, from your dream state it is an amazing, and very different awareness from the other techniques I have already mentioned. And it is just as real and just as valuable to receive information and knowledge.

Anything and everything is absolutely possible in the waking physical state. For some it is difficult to accept the totality of that statement. However, most can easily accept that anything and everything is absolutely possible in the dream state. In the dream state all the laws of the physical reality do not apply. You can absolutely communicate with your loved ones in your dreams. Without training, sometimes it is real, sometimes it is a creation in your dreams - either of an aspect of you or an aspect of them. With training, usually one hypnosis session, you can easily visit with the actual Souls of your departed loved ones on the Other Side through dream control. When using dream control properly, you have unlimited access to the infinite power of your mind and it is much easier to do the 'impossible'.

When I do group sessions specifically to bring all attendees to the Other Side everyone has an amazing experience. Seeing, feeling, hearing, their loved ones, their Spirit Guides face to face. Everyone receives valuable information and knowledge about themselves, their loved ones, their life, and their path. They all have their questions answered directly.

On rare occasions, usually if the person did not follow the pre-hypnosis instructions, and/or they want the experience so bad, they may allow their conscious mind to interfere. For those individuals, even though they still get to have an amazing experience, I recommend a private session. In the group session I continue to guide the attendees higher and higher aware through several levels. I do this to ensure the best I can, that everyone reaches the heights we want. In the private session, however, I am able to gage exactly where the client is and I am able to guide the client where she wants, or needs, to go. If I discover that the client's conscious mind is interfering too much, I quickly get the client to allow the conscious mind to let go with several rapid hypnotic techniques. Knowing that whatever is experienced with their higher states of awareness will be shared with their conscious mind, clients let go enough to have the beautiful experience without any interference.

When you get to the Other Side, many times, you are enjoying the experience so much, the energy, the love, the bliss, that the questions you had prior to reaching these heights are no longer important to you. Sometimes, although enjoying where they are, they are going to the Other Side to visit someone specific. People forget that they can ask their Spirit Guides if their loved one is available and if it is ok to visit with them at that moment. Sometimes they are busy or just not available. In a private session I am able to guide the client more to ask the necessary questions.

After going through the 2-Day Healing Workshop & Evolve Your Soul Training, and continuing to practice remote healing by connecting to Source, I introduce another technique to easily and instantly bring you to the Other Side. I train and program you to instantly connect with your Super-

Conscious mind, the observer part of who you are, to accomplish amazing goals and powerfully heal on every level. After this particular training you have a skill set to instantly connect to your Super-Conscious mind, and with pre-programmed key words combined with your intention, for you to be on the Other Side in any number of ways, with many variations of perceptions and awareness.

When I first started doing any type of session to visit the Other Side, whether in a private or a group setting, I discovered one possible obstacle that occasionally interfered with having the amazing experience. With certain individuals they would be in their own way because of certain offenses, or perceived offenses, they may have committed. These individuals needed to be forgiven of all prior offenses before they would allow themselves to reach the Other Side with their current consciousness.

The Other Side is a beautiful area of Pure Love, no judging, no ego, Perfect Healing, and ABSOLUTE FORGIVENESS! Although, whether you believe you need to be forgiven, or not, before you journey there, you truly do not. Once you arrive on the Other Side you instantly receive perfect healing FORGIVENESS! However, when you attend either a private session or a group workshop to visit the Other Side I will always do a complete and powerful forgiveness session with you prior to doing the Other Side session. You will absolutely be forgiven for anything you have ever done in this life, past lives, and anything you may do in the future, intentionally or unintentionally. You will be free from any negative

Karma from that session. You will be guided to rip up any negative Karmic agreements, making all, if any, Karmic contracts null and void. These sessions are so very freeing and healing, allowing you to be the perfect you and allowing you to easily visit the Other Side with extreme clarity.

In my 2-Day Healing Workshop & Evolve Your Soul Training I instruct you to travel to the Other Side instantly through self-hypnosis. From the workshop going forward you easily master the ability to visit the Other Side anytime you wish, under any circumstances, to heal yourself or others, to visit with loved ones, to gain knowledge and information from your Spirit Guides, and to powerfully create your reality. I also offer private sessions for you to train in astral traveling, dream control, channeling and much more. After the 2-Day Healing Workshop, and my National Hypnosis Certification course I offer a Master Healer's program for those of you who wish to teach others how to easily heal and to master several variations of Pure Love healing, and with channeling God's energy through your physical hands for healing. I also train you to instantly connect with your super-conscious mind for the most amazing benefits for yourself and others.

There are infinite ways in which you can gain access to the Other Side. Each technique I teach you also has infinite variations. There are no limits! There are also infinite variations in how you can and will communicate with loved ones and your Spirit Guides. I can tell you, or any one of my students and clients can tell you, how amazing and beautiful the Other

Side is. Words, however, can only express a fraction of the beauty of visiting the Other Side.

Imagine the happiest feeling you have ever felt in your entire life and combine that feeling with the most amount of love you have ever felt, and multiply those combined feelings by a million, and that feeling is only a fraction of what you feel when you are on the Other Side. Now imagine along with that feeling you begin to understand the great mysteries with amazing clarity. Imagine unlocking all of your infinite potential to transcend the physical laws and shift your awareness to heights you may have never dreamed possible. All of this and so much more is available to you when you visit the Other Side!

CHAPTER 11: VISIT NOW!

"It is beyond doubt that all our knowledge begins with experience."

- Immanuel Kant

"Let go of any limitations, there are none. Allow yourself to move from states of doubt and step into a powerful state of Knowing."

- Geozuwa

Are you excited to know that there is more to this life than just this life? Are you excited to know that you are eternal and death is not the end? There is life after death! This life you are experiencing now, even a hundred years, is just a blink of an eye. Are you excited to discover that you too can have amazing and powerful abilities without having a near death experience? You can visit and communicate, directly, with your loved ones who have passed. It is simple and easy to reach the Other Side in your current life without dying. Do you want to go?

Every person who has done these sessions with me come back from their visit renewed. Each has a brand new view of this world. The biggest problems they thought they had before visiting the Other Side now seem so trivial. They received the answers and the guidance they needed. Each person has a new awareness, knowing that we come from this beautiful loving world and we return to that perfect place of love, joy, and complete happiness when we depart this life. The Other Side is our real home.

In this physical world when you are away from home, even a little amount of time, you miss it. You will call family members, friends, and the people you love, several times, even if you are away for only a few nights. What about extended trips? Do you Skype with family members, children, spouses, and friends?

We leave our true home, on the Other Side, when we are born into this world. In the west our current life span is about eighty years. Imagine being away from your current home, from your loved ones, your entire lifetime without ever getting a chance to even call. Never knowing anything about them or when you will see them again.

That is the feeling of emptiness, some report, not knowing where it is coming from. You are away from your true home. Yes, you may very well be traveling with your family from the Other Side, in this life - they may even be your family in this life, but you do not even know it. I am here to tell you it is nonsense to think you have to wait to die to call or visit your family or home! You can do it now in this life! We were not designed to be away from home for a hundred years, to live with amnesia, not having any access to communicate. You have all of the tools and equipment necessary to do so!

There is no reason to wait. There are infinite reasons why you should visit now! You may think that reading this book, and perhaps so many other books on this subject, is enough to believe and accept that there is life after death. Maybe you have always had a firm belief, faith, that there is a magnificent and perfect place where we go when we die. Is believing and having faith enough? Perhaps.

Back in the 1800's there was a chap named Napoleon who was conquering all of Europe. In one particular battle, in Russia, he was separated from his troops. The Russian soldiers were hot on his trail. He was being chased through a small town and finally gave them the slip by running into a tailor shop. Napoleon implored the proprietor to hide him. The man knew that if he did not, and the French won the battle he would be in trouble. If he did hide Napoleon and the Russians win the battle he would be in trouble. The man decided to hide him under a pile of clothing on the floor.

The Russian soldiers entered the shop demanding the whereabouts of Napoleon. The tailor said that he was not there. The soldiers went around the shop searching anyway. With the bayonets at the ends of their rifles they were poking, and stabbing at the pile of clothes on the floor. Disgruntled, the soldiers left.

After the French won the battle they entered the shop. Napoleon emerged from the pile of clothing to greet his soldiers. The tailor approached Napoleon and asked, "How did it feel to be so close to death?" Napoleon yelled, "I am the Emperor of Europe! How dare you address me! This man must be executed at once! And I will give the command!"

The tailor was taken aback. He had just saved Napoleon's life. Now he was being tied to the post by the soldiers and blind folded. The man was trembling with fear. His heart was pounding uncontrollably. He thought of all the things he wanted to do in life and never got the chance to do. He thought about his wife, his family, with complete sadness - he knew he would never see them again. How would they fair in this world without him? The man was on the verge of tears, shaking, and trembling as Napoleon shouted, "Ready." As the man heard the rifles clicking, "Aim", the man's heart beating out of his chest, perspiring in buckets, gasping in a final breathe of terror anticipating the bullets. Hearing little footsteps approaching him, wondering what was going on, Napoleon lifted the tailor's blind fold and said, with a smile, "That's how it feels."

Napoleon knew the value of experience. For one to truly know what something is like one must experience it! To truly know that something is real you must experience it for yourself! You can have a great undeniable faith that something is real and that is wonderful. But it will always be faith, even if you claim to 'know'.

Yes, this is an absolute invitation for you to visit the Other Side and experience it NOW! This is an invitation to no longer be in doubt. This is an invitation to confirm the reality of your eternal Soul. You no longer have to live in fear of any kind. Be free! Now is the time for you to step out of the darkness and live in the light. To wake up! To realize your true infinite potential! Allow your awareness to grow beyond what "they" in the physical world tell you is real or possible. Now is your time to be happy, and to let go of the anchors of the old belief systems. Now is your time to enjoy life to the fullest! Now is your time to discover your true infinite and eternal nature - who you are. Now is the time to visit the Other Side!

Remember you do not have to die to enter Heaven. You can visit the Other Side as many times as you wish while you are alive and I will assist you with immense gratitude!

DISCLAIMER FOR HEALING:

Although I am absolutely certain of how powerful your mind is and I know that most, if not all, ailments or health issues are influenced, caused, triggered, or controlled by your mind, and it is possible for you to instantly heal any and all issues using your mind and/or the Infinite Pure Love Healing Energy from the Source of all Creation, or the Infinite Energy within yourself, I am not telling you not to go to the Doctor or to seek medical opinions and treatment. One of the main ingredients for healing is for you to believe. Believe it! Expect it! Know it! It does not have to be a difficult road to believe or to be in a state of knowing, but for some it is. Until you know with absolute certainty how easy it is to be healed, to heal yourself; please seek medical assistance.

Your immune system is perfect and you should remain healthy at all times. If you do begin to have an ailment, a discomfort, a pain, treat it as a message that something, other than the symptom, needs to be corrected. Ask yourself if you are holding on to any negative thought patterns such as anger, fear, guilt, shame, or inadequacy. Ask yourself if you are remaining in certain situations you know you should not be in. Are you allowing toxic people with unhealthy behavior and negative attitudes to stay in your life and effect your moods and thoughts in any way? There are many questions to ask yourself to examine what needs to be changed or corrected. And there are infinite possibilities as to what the cause of the ailment may be. The ailment, the discomfort, or the pain may not be yours. Your sub-conscious mind, your super-conscious mind, and your Spirit Guides know all of the answers to the questions and what needs to be adjusted for you to attain and maintain perfect health.

CDs offered by Geozuwa:

CHAKRA HYPNOSIS

DREAM CONTROL HYPNOSIS CD SERIES:
Dream Control 1
Dream Control 2
Dream Control: Self-Healing
Dream Control: Astral Travel
Dream Control: The Other Side
Dream Control: Super Part
Dream Control: Spirit Guides

INNER TEMPLE OF CREATION:
Creating Your Temple
Creating Your Reality
Creating Your Day
Developing Your Psychic Abilities
Healing Mind, Body, and Soul
Perfect Health
Attracting Money
Super Part
The Other Side
Remote Healing 1 & 2(exclusive for attendees of 2-Day
Healing Workshop)

SELF-LOVE & APPRECIATION

For a complete description of these CDs and other
information please visit:
www.AscendedHealer.com

Up-coming Workshops and Trainings offered by Geozuwa:

*THE OTHER SIDE
* AURA
* 2-DAY HEALING WORKSHOP & EVOLVE YOUR
  SOUL TRAINING
* CHANNELING
* DREAM CONTROL
* ASTRAL TRAVEL TRAINING
* NATIONAL HYPNOSIS CERTIFICATION
* NLP CERTIFICATION
* PAST LIVES/FUTURE LIVES/LIFE BETWEEN LIVES

For more information and dates on up-coming workshops and events please visit:

www.AscendedHealer.com

CPSIA information can be obtained at www.ICGtesting.com
Printed in the USA
LVOW04s0510180615

442912LV00003B/4/P